POLYMER
CLAY BEADS

POLYMER CLAY BEADS

TECHNIQUES • PROJECTS • INSPIRATION

Grant Diffendaffer

LARK BOOKS

A Division of
Sterling Publishing Co., Inc.
New York / London

Senior Editor: Valerie Shrader
Line Editor: Fran Ross
Associate Editor: Nathalie Mornu
Art Director: Megan Kirby
Cover Designer: Cindy LaBreacht
Associate Art Director: Shannon Yokeley
Assistant Designer: Travis Medford
Art Production Assistant: Jeff Hamilton
Editorial Assistance: Dawn Dillingham,
Kathleen McCafferty, Cassie Moore
Illustrator: Orrin Lundgren
Project Photographer: Stewart O'Shields
Hands-on Photographer: Nick Elias
Cover Photographer: Grant Diffendaffer

Publication Data

ects - inspiration / Grant Diffendaffer.--

p. cm.
Includes bibliographical references and index.
ISBN 1-60059-024-1
1. Beadwork. 2. Beads. 3. Silverwork. I. Title.
TT860.W33 2006
745.58'2--dc22

2006001618

10 9 8 7 6 5 4 3 2 1

First Edition

Published by Lark Books, A Division of
Sterling Publishing Co., Inc.
387 Park Avenue South, New York, N.Y. 10016

Text © 2007, Grant Diffendaffer
Photography © 2007, Lark Books unless otherwise specified
Illustrations © 2007, Lark Books unless otherwise specified

Distributed in Canada by Sterling Publishing,
c/o Canadian Manda Group, 165 Dufferin Street
Toronto, Ontario, Canada M6K 3H6

Distributed in the United Kingdom by GMC Distribution Services,
Castle Place, 166 High Street, Lewes, East Sussex, England BN7 1XU

Distributed in Australia by Capricorn Link (Australia) Pty Ltd.,
P.O. Box 704, Windsor, NSW 2756 Australia

The written instructions, photographs, designs, patterns, and projects in
this volume are intended for the personal use of the reader and may be
reproduced for that purpose only. Any other use, especially commercial
use, is forbidden under law without written permission of the copyright
holder.

Every effort has been made to ensure that all the information in this book
is accurate. However, due to differing conditions, tools, and individual
skills, the publisher cannot be responsible for any injuries, losses, and
other damages that may result from the use of the information in this
book.

If you have questions or comments about this book, please contact:
Lark Books
67 Broadway
Asheville, NC 28801
(828) 253-0467

Manufactured in China

ISBN 13: 978-1-60059-024-5
ISBN 10: 1-60059-024-1

For information about custom editions, special sales, premium and
corporate purchases, please contact Sterling Special Sales Department
at 800-805-5489 or specialsales@sterlingpub.com.

CONTENTS

POLYMER CLAY is a marvel. The first time I held a polymer bead in my hand I found myself in wonder at the depth of detail and the skill it took to make the bead. This material awakened my creativity as nothing else had. As soon as I laid my hands on it, I knew I would work with it for a very long time. Its responsiveness allows you to realize a vast range of creative visions. Though versatile, it is still clay, and has its own way of moving. It flows and is responsive to forces in a geologic fashion, incrementally, over time, and in different ways, in different states.

Because I had such an affinity for the material, I soon found myself deep in a pursuit that was to become my life's path. I quickly graduated from beads to making vessels and other larger pieces. In more recent years, I've returned to working with beads, and I'm still fascinated with how much can be done in such a little space. A bead is a small canvas, but a space in which there are a myriad of possibilities for you to express yourself in form, color, and pattern.

Researchers believe the oldest beads to be 100,000-year-old shells with holes drilled through them that were found in Algeria and Israel. Beads since then have been made from seedpods, stones, and many other naturally occurring forms that lend themselves to stringing. Take a lesson from a natural decorative shape such as a snowflake—each similar to the next, yet unique. No matter how hard you try to make them the same, each bead in a set will vary from the others. There are too many variables and too many choices along the way for it to be otherwise. So polymer beads are the perfect medium to systematically explore variations in form.

INTRODUCTION

If you perfect the tutorials in this book, you'll be able to make beads much like the ones I make. Further, you can incorporate the skills into your own work. I introduce you to seven different categories of beads. The first, simple hand-formed beads, are easily made with few tools, but offer infinite variations. Pearlized mica-clay beads showcase the dazzling chatoyant effects this clay exhibits, while textured beads incorporate an intriguing surface that provides both tactile and visual pleasures. Lathe-turned beads present the opportunity to shape raw or cured clay in countless ways. Recursive molded beads are created in stages, with each phase in the process extending an invitation to alter the final product. Molded hollow-form beads are light as a feather, and mandrel-formed pillow beads are designed specifically to grace the neck. The beads are presented in succession, as some of the techniques build upon one another, and many of the categories include variations.

I hope you will learn something much more important than the mere mechanics, though; I want

this book to empower you to approach your own creative endeavors without fear of the outcome. Each of the beads in this book was produced after many dead ends, yet I consider my unrealized pieces not failures but educational opportunities. I pick up the clay for the sake of engaging in the creative process. I do it for that sacred moment of revelation when the clay emerges transformed. Keep in mind the master potter who would every year smash his favorite pot to bits to remind himself of the importance of non-attachment. A crucial stumbling block to artistic creativity is over-attachment to the forms we have created. Don't be afraid to fail.

I've also included a gallery of work from my peers. The work of these artists, as various as it is, has one thing in common. Each bead is the distillation of a mature creative vision. Let these pieces inspire you. On a personal level, Pier Voulkos was a great influence on my creative path. Through her efforts as an inspirational artist, a meticulous craftsperson,

a warm and funny person, and an engaging and generous teacher, she has done a great deal to bring polymer to the art world at large. Her work, and that of Mike Buesseler, introduced me to the world of mica-clay techniques and laid the foundation for that chapter in this book. Pier's influence can be seen particularly in the sections on Carved-Ingot Beads and Veneered Pillow Beads.

Pier once told me to be fearless. I hope I can pass that lesson on to you. Be fearless: Experiment with these techniques in your own way, and try other "crazy" ideas in new and random ways just to see what happens. Have fun, and in the process, learn about the clay. Dive into it, play with it. Squish it, squash it, squeeze it, roll it out, roll it up, stack it up, cut it down, slice it, slam it, smash it, stretch it, turn it, twist it, cut it, chop it, bake it, bend it, break it, carve it, grind it, reduce it, reuse it, mold it, mash it, poke it, prod it, tease it, finesse it, and of course, polish it. Oh, and one more thing (something else I learned from Pier): Own it.

THE BASICS

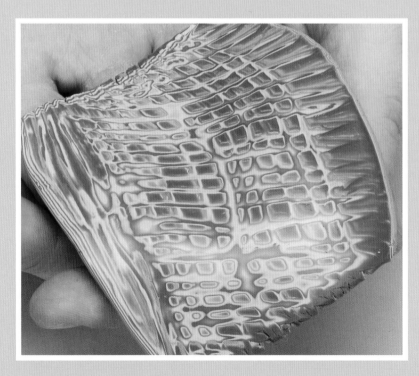

This book introduces you to the many types of beads you can create with versatile polymer clay. Although this book assumes some familiarity with the medium, here's the essential information you need to work with the material.

POLYMER CLAY PRIMER

Polymer clay is a synthetic, oven-hardening modeling material, made from polyvinyl chloride, or PVC. It is combined with dyes for color and a plasticizer to make it malleable. Polymer clay can be manipulated in an infinite variety of ways. When heated at temperatures easily achievable with a home oven, it hardens, and then can be further manipulated by lathe turning, sawing, carving, drilling, sanding, and buffing. It is phenomenal for making beads.

Most art stores and even some variety stores with an art department sell polymer clay. While you may chance upon a savvy brick-and-mortar store that meets your needs, the easiest way to find an educated retailer, quality selection, and good prices is online. Specialty retailers such as those found on the Internet are also a great source of information about polymer clay and polymer clay tools.

Clay Varieties

There is no single best polymer clay. Each clay has strengths and weaknesses, and what might be considered a weakness in one instance can be a strength in another. The best clays are multi-purpose. The clay you use is largely a matter of personal preference. Art suppliers oriented toward polymer clay are an excellent source of advice on which clays are suited for special tasks.

Conditioning

Polymer clay must be conditioned in order to be easily manipulated in its raw state and to achieve full strength when cured. You may do this by hand, but using a pasta machine, which rolls the clay into manageable sheets, is preferable. To condition your clay, slice the block and run the slices through the pasta machine. Combine the slices into a larger sheet and run that through again. Double the sheet over and run it through

(fold first, so as not to trap air bubbles). Repeat this process until the clay is of smooth and even consistency, with no holes or bubbles, and relatively even edges. Then, run it through another half-dozen times (about the same amount of rolling it takes to thoroughly blend two colors together). Occasionally folding the clay, and running it through with the seam on either the left or right, will help to even out and square up the sheet.

In the end, you want your clay to be bubble free, as bubbles can cause cracking and bumps on the surface of your finished bead. You can pop bubbles with a needle tool. Mostly, though, they can be worked to the surface by repeated conditioning of the clay. Conditioned clay can be used immediately for techniques that require softer clay, or can be left to sit for some time to firm up. Conditioned clay that sits unused for too long may need to be conditioned again to be easily usable. Another option to get stiff clay moving again is to gently warm it using a warm tile on a heating pad.

Changing Clay Consistency

Polymer clay varies in consistency, from soft and mushy to stiff and crumbly. Sometimes you will need to adjust the consistency of the clay to make it suitable to your work. Crumbly clay can be softened by mixing in additives designed for this purpose. Overly soft clay can be made firm and more manageable by leaching it: simply press a sheet between two pieces of plain paper. Burnish the paper using a flexible plastic card, such as an old library card, to ensure full contact between paper and clay. Using thinner sheets of clay means that for a given volume, more surface area is in contact with the paper, and the clay releases more plasticizer more quickly.

Curing

Polymer clay is baked, or "cured," to harden it. Each brand of clay must be raised to a specific temperature for a specific amount of time relative to the thickness of the clay. Following the manufacturer's instructions, use a quality oven and oven thermometer to ensure proper curing. Convection ovens seem to be the most reliable, as the circulating air keeps them more evenly heated. Toaster ovens heat in a particularly uneven fashion.

Polymer clay may begin to harden above about 110°F (43°C) and does not require much exposure to high heat before it hardens. Hardening and curing are two different things though. If you want your beads to be durable and long lasting, then you must not only choose the right clay for the job and properly construct your creation, but it must also be fully cured.

Polymer clay cures at a range of temperatures, mostly at about 265 to 275°F (129 to 135°C). This means the clay can be cured in a home oven. Common sense dictates, however, that you use a dedicated oven for your clay (an oven that you don't use for food). While the clay is labeled nontoxic, the plasticizer will condense in your oven, is likely to burn off at higher temperatures, and could find its way into your food.

As for the toxicity of the clay, a recent university study suggests that when consumed in large amounts, the plasticizer has an effect on the body similar to that of cholesterol. So don't eat it! More important, though, don't burn it, which can release irritating fumes and smoke. Hydrogen chloride is created when clay burns, at around 400°F (204°C), and creates hydrochloric acid when it makes contact with water. You won't dissolve your water-based self if you burn a few beads, but there will certainly be a stench! Burned beads are a great reason for an oven thermometer, a quality oven, and ventilation. While you don't have to install a vent hood or fan, at least keep your oven near a window that you can open.

ESSENTIAL TOOLS

For many years I worked with very few tools—a jar for a roller and a wallpaper blade to slice the clay. I was as happy as a clam until I found out about pasta machines. As soon as I had a pasta machine I was as happy as at least two clams! Suddenly I could quickly and easily create a variety of sheets of even thickness. Then I got a motor for the pasta machine and was able to condition and make sheets of clay much more quickly, have both hands free, and work easily with much larger sheets of clay. There will always be more tools to make your life easier and expand the number of things you can do with clay. If you are on a budget though, wait to get more tools until you have a job that is not possible to do with your current tools, or when the time saved is worth more to you than the money spent.

Basic polymer clay tools

● **Pasta machine**

These are available from cooking stores and businesses that supply polymer clay tools, and are essential to quickly and easily condition your clay and roll it into consistent, even sheets. Some pasta machines label the thickest setting with the highest number; others, with the lowest. In this book, I refer to settings as "thickest," "thinnest," "medium," or relative to these, such as "one up from the thinnest."

Miscellaneous items used in bead making, such as brushes and trimming tools

● **Sharp blades**

These come in many forms. Medical tissue blades are flexible and at least a sharp as any other blade. They will oxidize, however, and may not hold a sharp edge for long. Various other blades are made exclusively for polymer clay. Some are long, some short, some flexible, and some are sharper than others. Some are made of stainless steel. Some are wave-shaped. My three main blades are a sharp flexible blade, a wavy blade, and an 8-inch (20.3 cm) floor stripper blade. These are available where you buy polymer clay.

● **A rolling pin**

I use a large acrylic rod that I bought at a plastics store, and an acrylic brayer from an art store. If you have nothing else, a jar works just fine.

● **An oven and an oven thermometer**

See the discussion of ovens on page 12.

The following tools and supplies are also used in this book. Depending on the techniques you wish to explore, you will need some—or all—of the following.

● **A hobby knife**

I suggest one with interchangeable blades.

● **A needle tool**

This can be as simple as a needle baked into a polymer handle.

● **A multi-purpose ball stylus or two**

These are great for making little holes.

● **A painter's palette knife**

This is perfect for removing clay stuck to your work surface.

Specialty tools, including a necklace mandrel and an extruder

- **Texture sheets**
  These indispensable items can be made in your studio from polymer clay, photopolymer resin, room temperature vulcanizing silicone (RTV), or natural latex rubber. You can also buy commercial texture sheets and rubber stamps for texturing applications.

- **Shaped clay cutters**
  Get various shapes and sizes. You will probably find circle cutters the most useful. I have a large 12-piece set that varies from about 1 to about 4½ inches (2.5 to 11.4 cm) in diameter. I mostly use the smaller ones. These cutters are available where you buy polymer and ceramic clay.

- **Various ring-shaped tools**
  I use nuts and bolts, washers, straws, tubes, pipes, etc., for impressing or cutting the clay.

- **Rubber-tipped clay shapers**
  These are available from ceramics supply stores.

- **A vegetable peeler (optional)**
  Polymer artist Dan Cormier has shown a specialized version to be useful in many ways.

- **A lathe**
  You may want to purchase an inexpensive lathe for turning and finishing beads. Get one with a chuck attached to the headstock to hold the bead mandrel. You will also want a rotating drill chuck for the tailstock. You can also create a makeshift lathe from a flex-shaft tool or variable-speed drill press. (My first lathe was an electric hand drill with an adapter that allowed me to mount the drill vertically—as a drill press—or horizontally. The simplest way to use it as a lathe was to simply drill a hole into the table top and then mount my mandrels with the tail end in this hole.) You can also set it up horizontally (like a typical lathe) with the tail end mounted in a hole drilled into a wall, desk,

- **A dedicated work surface**
  Glass is excellent, as its smooth surface will leave all of your clay smooth. If you use glass without beveled edges, be sure to tape the edges so you don't cut yourself. Acrylic works fine too, but cutting blades will scratch it, and the scratches are liable to make marks on raw clay. You can remove much of the roughness and scratches from an acrylic surface by scraping it with a floor-stripper blade.

- **A linoleum-carving tool**
  Be sure to get one with various cutting bits, available in the printmaking section of your art supply store.

or other vertically mounted piece of wood. (My current lathe is an inexpensive hobby lathe with a rotating drill chuck on the tailstock; I have modified it to hold the handpiece of my flex-shaft tool. The handpiece acts as the headstock of the lathe and provides the turning power.)

- **Ceramic trimming tools**
  Use these with a lathe. I use the highest-quality tools I can find, bought at a dedicated ceramics supply house. They cost more but are sharper and longer lasting.
  ⅛-inch (3 mm) steel rod cut into mandrels. (See tutorial later in this chapter, on page 27). These are at the heart of my lathe-turning and textured-bead techniques.

- **A heavy-duty extruder**
  These are available where you buy polymer clay. They're great for making canes and for extruding multipurpose finned shapes such as stars, which are beautiful when turned on the lathe. Dies of various shapes and sizes will be helpful.

- **A tabletop press**
  I use a simple press that I made by mounting two inexpensive, light-duty woodworkers' vises on a wooden box, so that a horizontal board rests on the bottom jaw of each. By cranking down on the clamps I can press anything I want between two boards. This is extremely useful for compressing clay with various molds, cutters, and texture sheets.

- **A lapidary belt sander**
  This tool is useful for removing large amounts of material from a piece of cured polymer. It's also great for shaping beads.

- **Dust mask**

- **Safety goggles**

- **A rasp**
  Made for woodworking, this file-like tool quickly removes large amounts of material, and

works well for shaping beads. With the rasp resting on your work surface, simply draw the bead across it.

- **Drywall screen in 80, 120, and 180 grit**
  This open abrasive screen removes material fast without clogging.

- **Sandpaper**
  Have on hand the following grits: 220, 320, 400, 600, 800, 1000, 1200, 1500.

- **A buffing wheel**
  See page 30 for more on buffing.

- **A flexible shaft machine**
  I find this tool invaluable, as most jewelers do. I use it to drive my lathe, drill, cut, and grind my beads.

- **A drill press**
  It's not really necessary if you have a flex shaft, but it's helpful for drilling beads otherwise. It can also be rigged up into a makeshift lathe or buffing wheel.

- **A dapping block**
  This tool is useful for making domed forms, molds of domed forms, etc.

- **A set of wooden dapping punches**
  Useful in conjunction with the dapping block, it's handy for hammering out bead caps, and as sculpture tools, mold-making tools, and more.

- **Steel dapping punches**
  I use these to create tube rivets. Tube rivets can protect the holes of polymer beads, and are also used to affix metal end caps. Get a set of 4-, 5-, and 6-mm punches.

- **A jewelry hammer**
  To aid in making tube rivets and end caps, use this tool.

- **A vibratory tumbler**

ESSENTIAL TECHNIQUES

In this section I'll explore some of the basic techniques I use to create polymer clay beads.

CREATING A "SKINNER BLEND"

Thanks to Judith Skinner, one of the pioneers in polymer clay, we have a simple way of creating gorgeous clay blends that transition smoothly from one color to another. You will probably use this indispensable technique every time you blend colors. The resultant gradient blends, known as Skinner blends, will help to bring an unparalleled depth and naturalness to your work.

STEP BY STEP

1. Start with two sheets of different colors rolled out on the thickest setting on your pasta machine.

2. Place one sheet on top of the other.

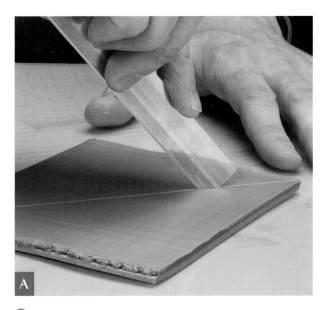

3. Lay a ruler diagonally from one corner to the other and slice through both sheets (photo A).

4. Assemble a new sheet from the resulting triangles that is half one color and half the other, and press the seam together with your fingertips (photo B).

5. Run your new sheet through the pasta machine (photo C).

6. Fold the sheet end to end. Put it through the pasta machine, fold first this time, keeping one color on your left and one on your right. Repeat until the colors are smoothly blended (photo D).

CREATING A CANE

Polymer clay is often manipulated using an ancient glass-working technique known as "millefiori,"

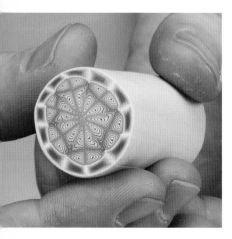

which means "thousand flowers" in Italian. In this technique, the clay is manipulated into rods, rolls, or "canes" of clay which have a consistent pattern from one end to the other, so that wherever you slice them, an identical cross-section is revealed. Millefiori is a simple way to create complex patterns and pictures that can be used as a veneer to pattern the surface of a bead, or turned in whole on a lathe.

This tutorial introduces the basic concept of canes. There are many "recipes" out there designed to yield specific results, but I prefer to offer a general recipe for success.

You can create canes by using your own color blends, design, and manner of assembly. You can distort, add to, and even remove clay from a cane in any fashion, as long as you follow one basic principle: Whatever you do to one part of the cane, you must do to the whole cane. This will ensure that your pattern remains consistent throughout, and will allow you to create precise and controlled patterns every time.

What follows is a tutorial for a simple millefiori cane. You will learn how to create a pattern, how to modify it, and, most important, how to use it in repetition to create highly ordered and symmetrical patterns.

STEP BY STEP

1. Begin by creating a Skinner blend of two colors. Cut an 8-inch-long (20 cm) sheet of the blended clay. Fold it in half and run it through the pasta machine sideways, on the thickest setting (one color goes in first; the other follows).

2. Create a 2-inch-long (5 cm) sheet of black clay on your thickest pasta machine setting.

3. Create a 2-inch-long (5 cm) sheet of white clay on your thickest pasta machine setting.

4. Lay the black sheet over the white (photo A) and run through the pasta machine, one setting up from the thinnest.

5. Lay the combined black-and-white sheet over the Skinner-blended sheet. Trim the ends so they are straight, and run the sheet through the pasta machine on the thickest setting (photo B).

6. Roll the sheet with your fingertips from one end to the other to create a simple "jellyroll" cane (photo C.) Gently but firmly roll the cane back and forth with your palms to seal the layers together. Take care not to distort the cane (photo D).

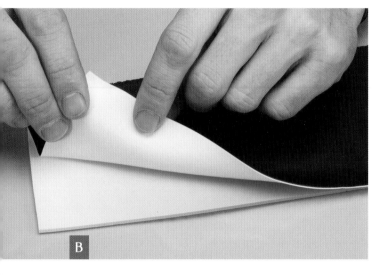

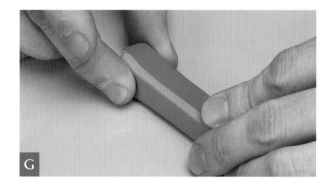

7. "Reducing" the cane involves stretching the cane, which shrinks the diameter, and all decorative elements contained within. Pinch your jellyroll on opposite sides to flatten the sides, and square it up (photo E). Place the cane against your work surface, and gently roll it with your brayer to flatten out the sides. Turn it and roll each side gently. Pinch the edges of the cane between the tips of your fingers and the work surface to refine the sharp edges on the corners (photo F). There will be an obvious line where the end of the jellyrolled clay sheet makes a seam on the outside of the cane. Keep this line, and any others you see, as straight as possible as you reduce the cane.

8. Pull the cane as you pinch it, gradually stretching it until it is 12 inches (31 cm) long. If you stretch the whole cane at once, it will reduce unevenly. Focus your reduction by separating your hands a bit at a time, reducing the cane bit by bit (photo G). When you are finished, the cane should be evenly thick along its whole length. Because the ends of a cane often become distorted during reduction, you can trim off the ends until you find an identical pattern on both ends.

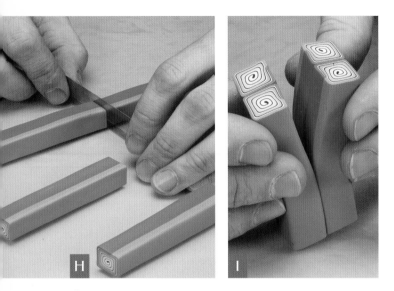

9. Cut the cane into four equal pieces, 3 inches (8 cm) each. Book-match the pieces so that when placed side by side, the pieces form a larger square cane with an identical symmetrical pattern on each end (photo H). As you assemble this larger cane, take care to match the lines down the sides of the smaller segments (photo I). This will ensure that the pattern comes together seamlessly through the length of the cane.

10. Pinch the cane together, and square it up, but do not reduce it yet (photo J). Set it aside.

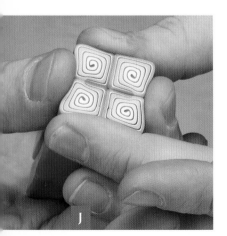

11. Make a 6-inch-long (15 cm) Skinner blend in a second set of colors. Roll this up into a jellyroll, with the

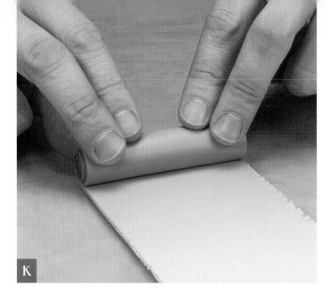

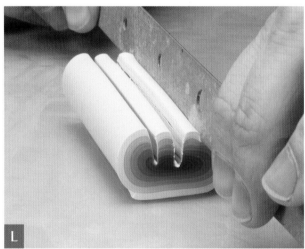

brighter color on the outside (photo K). Use a ruler or some other fine-edged object to make several lengthwise impressions in one side of the cane. Keep the impressions parallel, of even depth (to about the middle of the cane), and straight down the cane from one end to the other (photo L). Pinch the cuts closed and square up the cane, taking care to keep the lines straight. Note how the impressions drag clay from the outside towards the middle of the cane—an excellent example of how you can distort a simple cane to create interest.

A similar technique is to pinch and pull an edge of a cane so that it stretches into thin line, then roll the sheet up; in short, you can systematically distort the cane along its length to create various patterns.

12. If necessary, reduce the new cane to 6 inches (15 cm) long and cut it in half. Book-match these halves to create a symmetrical pattern.

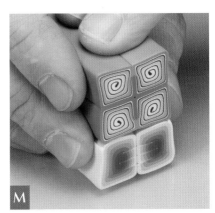

13. Place the first cane on top of the second, forming a new cane (photo M).

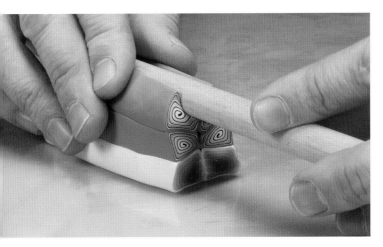

14. Using a dowel, pen, or other cylindrical object, make an impression along the length of the first cane segment. Draw the corners up around the dowel (photo N).

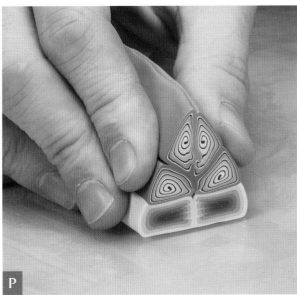

15. Remove the dowel and bring the two corners together in a point. The cane is now triangular (photos O and P).

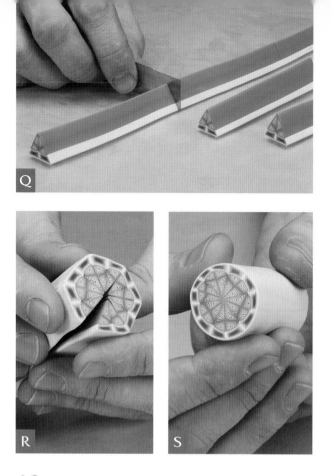

16. Reduce the cane. Gradually remove any curvature from the edges. Be sure to close up any remaining space where you brought the cane around the dowel. Equalize the triangle so that all sides are of the same length, but don't do this all at once. You will do a more accurate job, with less overall distortion, if you gradually even up the sides as you reduce the cane.

17. Trim off the distorted ends and cut the remaining cane into six equal lengths of at least 3 inches (8 cm) each (photo Q). Assemble the triangular canes into a hexagonal cane, taking care to make all lines within line up. Compress the cane; roll it on your work surface to remove the edges and round it out. Reduce it to your desired size by rolling and stretching (photos R and S).

CREATING A MOKUME GANE PATTERN

Mokume gane is a Japanese metalworking technique that translates as "wood-grained metal." Transferred to polymer clay, the technique involves stacking sheets of colored clay, distorting the stack, and then cutting into it, revealing the pattern within. This technique will work with as few as two layers of clay. As the number of layers increases, so do the possible variations. Thin slices of the mokume gane pattern can be used to decorate beads. Beads can also be formed directly from thicker blocks or "ingots" of mokume gane. What follows is one variation of the mokume gane technique.

STEP BY STEP

1. Choose two different colors of clay. Try one dark and one light, or one warm and one cold color. Choose colors that stand out clearly against one another.

2. Roll out a 3-inch (8 cm) sheet of each color on the thickest pasta machine setting.

3. Layer two contrasting colors and run them through on the thickest setting.

4. Cut the sheet in half and stack one half on the other. Run the four-layer sheet through on the thickest setting.

5. Fold the sheet in half and run it through the machine again. It is now eight layers thick.

6. Fold the sheet in half again and run it through the machine one setting down from the thickest. Fold the sheet over again and roll it gently with a rod or brayer to seal the two layers together.

7. Using a texture plate or rubber stamp or other implement, impress a pattern into the clay. Remember to use an appropriate release to prevent the clay from sticking in your texture plate. Water works for Premo and Kato clays; cornstarch works for Fimo (but the scraps will retain the starch and make for weaker clay—keep these for scrap clay only).

8. Remove thin slices of the texture by bending your blade and slicing parallel to your work surface (photo T).

9. Run the mokume gane sheet through the pasta machine on progressively thinner settings until it is smooth. If it becomes too thin to handle, apply a thin sheet of clay to the back (photo U).

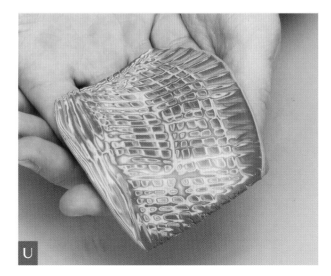

- Experiment, experiment, experiment! Create patterns you never would have imagined. Distort your canes. Press them along their length with dowels, rulers, rollers, or other rigid tools. Turn your triangle canes into square canes, your square canes into triangles, then circles, and back again. Simple patterns become much more exciting when you cut them in half and match the two pieces together to create symmetry.

- You can always reduce a cane further, but it's difficult to accurately enlarge it.

- Canes are most easily reduced with precision when they are shaped like triangles or squares. Round canes can also be reduced fairly precisely, but with somewhat more difficulty.

- Your cane will reduce more evenly if your clay is consistently soft. If one piece of clay is softer, you can firm it up by "leaching" out the plasticizer: Roll your clay out in thin sheets and sandwich it between sheets of plain paper with a weight, such as a book, on top. When the plasticizer has leached into the paper (the paper looks wet or oily), test the clay to see if it has firmed up. Repeat until your clay is of the desired consistency.

- Some brands of clay are softer than others. While this makes them easier to manipulate, it also makes them more prone to accidental distortion. Firmer clays hold their shape better and create more precise canes that are easier to slice. Some people cane with clay as it comes out of the package; others leach the clay or mix two different brands together.

- Heat and manipulation also soften the clay. If you find your cane becoming too soft or sticky to work with, let it rest for a while and firm up. You can even put it in the freezer for a bit.

- To minimize distortion when you slice the cane, use the sharpest blade you can find. I prefer medical tissue blades.

SPECIAL TECHNIQUES

Some of the organic results I obtain are from the use of the following specialized techniques.

USING TEXTURE PLATES

I could write a whole book on texture plates, which you can use to texture your beads by rolling the beads across them, pressing the beads between them, or stretching them to conform to a mold. A texture plate can be used either to create replicas of one texture, or as a basis to improvise on variations of a texture. It can be used with mica clays to create a "ghost image," or the illusion of texture where there is only a smooth surface. You can produce a whole range of effects from using just one texture sheet on a mokume gane sheet or block of clay. Using recursive molding, you can transform a texture into a vast array of fascinating three-dimensional forms.

There are numerous types of texture plates, each with their own special characteristics and unique ways of affecting the clay. While most texture sheets serve multiple purposes, nothing beats the right texture sheet for the job.

Polymer Clay Texture Plates

The simplest way to create a texture plate is with polymer clay itself. Such a plate is suitable for making ghost images but will not provide the precise, even impression necessary for a perfectly smooth, uniformly high-contrast ghost image with fine detail. Impressions can, however, be made very deep, resulting in bold contrasts in the ghost image. They can be used for mokume gane, as the foundation of the patterning process in the Textured Beads section (page 58), and to make flexible latex texture sheets like those used in the Recursive Molded Beads chapter (page 90). The beauty of these plates is that they are low-tech, easy to make, and immediately gratifying. They can be sculpted and embellished in detail. Beginning with a photopolymer plate, rubber stamp, or other commercial texture sheet, while not necessary, will allow you to quickly build a library of patterns.

To make a texture plate, you need a 10-inch (25 cm) sheet of scrap clay; texture plates; rubber stamps, etc. (optional); small objects to press into the clay such as a ball stylus, twine, string, and straws; and a linoleum carving tool.

STEP BY STEP

1. Condition scrap clay and roll out a sheet on your thickest pasta machine setting. Double it over to form a sheet approximately 5 x 5 inches (13 square cm).

2. Use your favorite texture implements to pattern approximately half the sheet. Try starting with a photopolymer plate, rubber stamp, or commercial texture sheet, and then embellish the texture with your ball stylus, pieces of twine that you impress into the surface to create curving lines, straw ends for tiny ring shapes, and other objects (photo A). You can also cut small holes with clay cutters that will make bold impressions excellent for ghost imaging. And you can use the clay cutters to make impressions in the texture sheet. Creating stripes of texture across the texture sheet will make patterns wrap around the

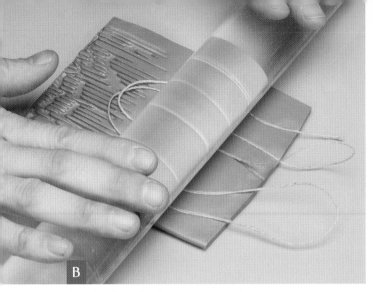

bead in bands. Leave spaces that you can come back to and carve with your linoleum tool after you cure the sheet (photo B).

3. Cure the sheet per the clay manufacturer's instructions.

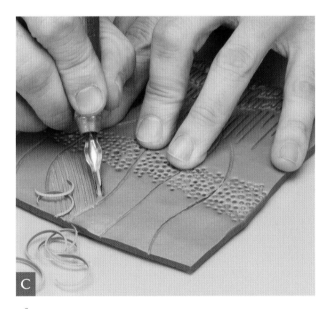

4. Using your linoleum-carving tool (I like the small V-gouge), carve your texture sheet until it is densely textured (photo C).

Photopolymer Texture Plates

Photopolymer texture plates allow you to efficiently turn a two-dimensional drawing, computer graphic, or photo into three-dimensional polymer art. These plates can be both relatively deep and precisely detailed—an excellent combination for ghost imaging, mokume gane, and texturing applications. Because they are clear, you can see when you have made an effective impression. They are an excellent foundation for making a number of different texture sheets.

Although I usually prefer to make them myself because it is less expensive and I have full control of the process, it can be messy and frustrating. It takes some experimentation to get the exposure correct and the exposure unit requires special training to build and operate. If you want to use texture plates to make beads, you will probably want to have a rubber stamp or flexographic plate maker make the actual photopolymer plates from artwork that you have created. (Photopolymer resin suppliers are good sources for plate makers.)

So you understand the entire process, photopolymer is an ultraviolet light-sensitive liquid resin, with a consistency of honey. During manufacture, the resin is sandwiched between sheets of glass, with a "negative" image on a transparency, and exposed to UV light. Where the light passes through the transparent areas of the image (the negative space), the resin hardens. Where blocked by the ink of the image, the resin stays liquid. After washing away the liquid resin, you are left with a plate bearing a three-dimensional relief of the original image. The resulting product can serve as a texture sheet, a flexographic printing plate, or a rubber stamp. So while you may choose to turn to a professional to create the actual plate, you can exercise your creativity when creating the design for the plates.

Preparing the Artwork

Your design must be composed entirely of black-and-white elements (no gray). The black elements become the etched-away portion of the texture plate, yielding raised elements in the clay. This surface texture is cut away to reveal a ghost image in mica clay. The white elements print clear on the transparency and harden into ridges on the plate, which in turn yield impressions in the clay.

The wider the mark on the transparency, the deeper the impression on the plate. Deeper impressions translate to bolder and more impressive ghost-image effects as well as the potential for more dramatic texturing applications.

Fine black line elements make shallow impressions on the plate, translating into shallow impressions in clay, which aren't much use for ghost imaging, mokume gane, or texturing applications, but which may work well for inking and other printing techniques. Creating a design with thin elements of negative space, or "white," in a sea of ink can lead to the washing away of the delicate exposed pieces with the still-liquid resin. Designs with many fine elements are generally more successful with a thinner and more shallowly etched stamp.

Despite not being able to complete the entire process yourself, it is an almost magical way to transform your own complex line art into three dimensions. There is nothing better if you want to make a detailed ghost image with high contrast and a perfectly smooth surface. It is also an excellent starting point for creating the polymer clay texture sheets described on page 24.

Flexible Texture Sheets

Flexible texture sheets can be bent and stretched to follow the contours of a curved bead, or even to create the contours of a curved bead, as with my recursive molding technique (see page 92).

Room-temperature vulcanizing silicone, or "RTV silicone" is a two-part mold-making material which

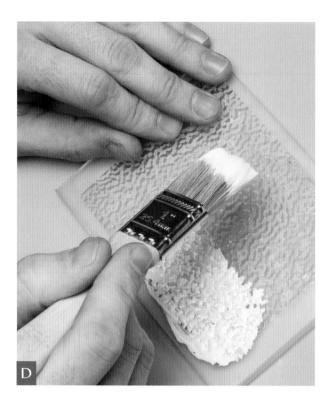

comes in both liquid and putty forms. Putty is easier to work with, and once mixed, it is pressed around an object to create a mold, or into another texture sheet (such as photopolymer or polymer clay) to create a flexible texture sheet. The putty sets in just a few minutes. These sheets are great for rolling textures onto beads with curved profiles, such as those turned on a lathe. RTV silicone is available from jewelry and sculpture supply shops.

Liquid latex rubber, available from art and sculpture supply shops, makes flexible, strong texture sheets ideal for recursive mold-making techniques. To create sheets, paint latex on a textured surface, such as a texture plate, and allow it to dry (photo D). Then add another coat. It takes several coats to make a thick-enough sheet with suitable strength. Latex takes longer to set up than RTV—approximately 48 hours. Because it is not as dense, latex creates sheets that won't make impressions as crisp or as deep as RTV. They are, however, very stretchy and can conform closely to complex surfaces.

CREATING TUBE BEADS

I make a big batch of plain tube beads at once, as a core for all my textured and many of my lathe-turned beads. This process can be varied to create tube beads with a beauty all their own. Try playing with colors. Try layering them with canes, swirling different colors together, using translucent clays, foils, or other inclusions.

STEP BY STEP

1. Condition and roll out a sheet of clay on the thickest setting of your pasta machine. The sheet should be as wide as your machine and about 8 to 12 inches (20 to 31 cm) long. The core will be covered with clay later but may be exposed again in the process, so use a color that will match your finished bead. This process will make a lot of tube beads. (There is no such thing as too many, and they are much easier to make in bulk!)

2. Trim one end so that you have a straight edge.

3. Lay a 12-inch (31 cm) steel mandrel (⅛-inch, or 3 mm, mild steel welding rod) across the end of the sheet, pinching up the leading edge to wrap it around the mandrel.

4. Roll the clay and mandrel forward, wrapping the whole sheet of clay around the mandrel (photo E). Take care not to trap any air bubbles as you roll. Trim off the outer end of the sheet at the point where the sheet began in the middle. This helps you roll tube beads of even thickness.

5. Roll the tube back and forth, applying even pressure from all sides, and gently pulling as you roll from the middle to the ends to stretch the tube to the length of the mandrel. You can also grasp the tube with your fingertips and pull and twist it back and forth. Do not push down on the ends of the mandrel as you roll, as this will widen the hole through the bead (photo F).

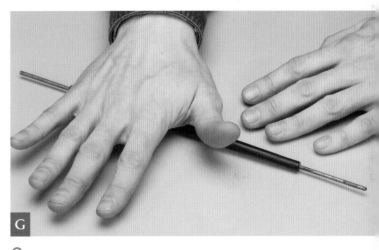

6. When the tube reaches the length of the mandrel, cut it in half around the middle. Remove half of the tube to roll later. Continue rolling the tube and repeating the process until you have a tube about ⅜ inch (1 cm) thick (photo G). Roll the tube with a piece of 36-grit sandpaper to texture the raw clay. This allows the clay to adhere to the surface when you later turn the bead into its finished form. Leaving the final tube on the mandrel, cut it into individual bead lengths (approx 1¼ inches, or 3 cm). The length of the core tube bead will determine the length of your finished bead.

7. Cure the tubes on the mandrel in the oven, per the clay manufacturer's instructions.

8. Remove the tubes from the mandrels while they are still warm (photo H).

Tips

Making bead mandrels

I cut my bead mandrels from ⅛-inch (.3 cm) mild steel wire welding rod that I buy at the local welding supply store. I cut it with an angle grinder, though you may cut it with a hacksaw, a cut-off wheel on a rotary tool, or some other device. I cut it to about 12 inches (30 cm) for rolling tube beads, and to about 6 inches (15 cm) for working on the lathe or rolling textured beads. Sand the ends with 220-grit sandpaper to remove sharp burrs. I also sometimes use 1/16-inch (.2 cm) mandrels, as in the section on Veneered Pillow Beads, on page 54, although they are flexible, and not suitable for the lathe-turning or bead-texturing techniques in this book.

ADHERING BEADS TO MANDRELS

I have tried many different ways of adhering beads to mandrels, which must be done to turn a bead with a mandrel on the lathe. The best way I have found is to essentially create a friction fit with the mandrel, by spraying the mandrel with a rubberizing solution designed to create a coating on tool handles.

STEP BY STEP

1. Spray an even coat over 3 to 4 inches (8 to 10 cm) in the middle of your mandrels.

2. After it dries, spray another coat, focusing more toward the middle of the mandrel.

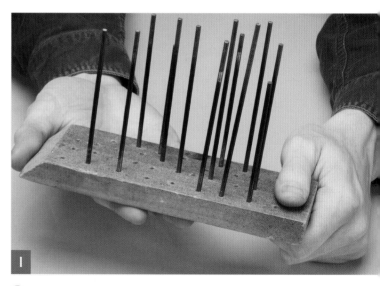

3. Repeat this process once or twice more (or as many times as necessary to achieve a friction bond with your bead) (photo I). After the rubber has dried, slide your bead into the middle of the mandrel. You may have to push on the bead with the end of the mandrel braced against another surface, such as your work surface. Be careful not to bend the mandrel as you push the bead on

J

(photo J). Your bead should fit snugly enough that it won't spin on the mandrel when you turn it on the lathe, yet not so snugly that you have to struggle to get it on the mandrel.

Tips

Making an oven stand for your beads

A simple stand can be made to bake many beads on mandrels at one time. Simply drill a piece of scrap wood with ⅛-inch-deep (.3 cm) holes in which to stand one end of each mandrel.

FINISHING TECHNIQUES

After you've created your beads, there is still finishing work to be done.

Sanding Beads by Hand

I use wet/dry sandpaper in the following grits: 220, 320, 400, 600, 800, 1000, 1200, and 1500. If you can't find these at your local hardware store, try an auto paint shop or jewelry supply store.

If you need to do a lot of shaping, you may want to start with a lapidary belt sander, a rasp, or drywall screen. If you only need to put a polish on a relatively refined surface, start with 400-grit sandpaper.

There are several effective ways to sand a bead by hand. To sand perfectly flat surfaces, place your sandpaper on a smooth work surface and move your bead against it (photo A). To sand curves, try placing a ½-inch-thick (1 cm) (or thicker) sponge under your sandpaper (photo B). Also try holding your bead in your dominant hand and cup the sandpaper in the other. Sand the bead by moving it

A

B

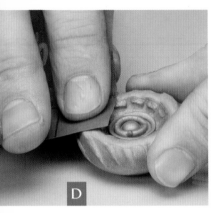

against the curved sandpaper surface (photo C).

For more delicate work, you may want to brace your bead against the table with one hand and use a small piece of sandpaper in your other hand (photo D). However you sand the bead, rinse it frequently in a bucket of water to remove buildup. Rinse your sandpaper regularly.

Finishing Beads on a Lathe

Using a lathe is a speedy way to give lathe-turned or textured beads a perfect finish. If your beads are rough, or require a lot of shaping, you may start with 80-grit (and then 120-grit) drywall screen. From there, move on to 220-grit wet/dry sandpaper. Holding a 2 x 2-inch (5 square cm) piece of sandpaper in your hand, press it gently against the turning bead (photo E). Wet the sandpaper and rinse it frequently to prevent buildup. You can also use a toothbrush or a sponge. Move through successive

grits, as high as you like. Don't skip grits, and be sure to thoroughly sand the bead with each grit to remove scratches from the previous one. You can stop as early as 600 grit, or go as high as 1500 for a glossier finish.

Tumbling Beads

Beads can be also be finished by using a vibratory tumbler. This update on the old-fashioned rock tumbler is used by rockhounds and jewelers alike, and can quickly put a nice shine on your beads. Vibratory tumblers are especially effective at polishing irregular surfaces. I have had success using plastic pellets as a tumbling media with successive tumbles of 220-, 400-, and 600-grit powders. Try experimenting with different tumbling media. You will find more information on media where you buy your tumbler.

Buffing

Always finish your sanded beads by washing them with a little dish detergent and water, and drying and buffing them. Buffing removes any dust or other coatings remaining after sanding and gives your beads a beautiful luster. You can give them a soft sheen by buffing them on your jeans, or on a soft cloth. For more shine, try using a piece of lamb's wool while they are turning on the lathe (photo F). Take care with buffing wheels. Muslin wheels can easily "burn" the surface of a polymer bead, requiring you to sand it again. Use unsown wheels on lower speeds. I use a lamb's-wool wheel that I bought at an auto paint store and mounted on a drill press.

Drilling and Piercing

Part of the beauty of polymer clay is that you can do much of the finishing in the raw state. Drilling the cured clay can be more precise, but it can stress the clay. If you can pierce your raw bead without damaging the surface and shape, then do it, as it will make a stronger hole. In some instances, you will build around a bead mandrel, thus eliminating the need to drill at all. Whether you pierce the raw clay with toothpicks, skewers, metal pins, or mandrels; or drill it cured, start with a small tool for each, creating a hole from each side and having them meet them in the middle. Increase tool size gradually until the hole is the size you need (photo G).

The strength of the hole varies depending on how you string the bead. Thicker, softer, and more flexible cord puts fewer demands on the hole. Thin stringing material with great tensile strength is more likely to cut into the edge of the bead

hole. The strongest holes are formed when the clay is raw and the surface outside the hole is approximately perpendicular (at a 90° angle) to the hole for about ⅛ inch (3 mm) before it curves back towards the other end of the bead. Avoid tapering away from the edge of the hole at more than a 45° angle.

Tips for Finishing

- Dry off your bead between sandings. You won't see any scratches or other surface details when the bead is wet. Learn what the surface looks like after being properly sanded with each grit. This is important to minimize the time re-sanding with lower grits to remove scratches.

- Use only wet/dry sandpaper from one manufacturer.

- Used sandpaper essentially acts at a higher grit than it did when it was new.

- Wear a dust mask when you use drywall screen, especially on the lathe. Ventilate your work area and clean up dust after work.

SIMPLE
HAND-FORMED
BEADS

Only the simplest tools are necessary to get rewarding results with polymer clay. The beads (and infinite variations) on the following pages can be created using nothing but a pasta machine, a sharp blade, a toothpick or skewer, and the metal lid of a jar—or similar small, smooth surface. The results are immediate, satisfying, and very likely to spark your imagination.

Grant Diffendaffer. *Bracelets,* 2007.
Each 10 inches (25 cm) long; beads 1
inch (3 cm) long. Hand-formed polymer
millefiori beads, elastic cord.

HANDMADE BEADS

To begin making simple handmade beads, you will need to create a pattern to decorate the core bead. You have many options. This tutorial focuses on patterning beads with cane slices or a thin veneer of mokume gane. For instructions on how to create these patterns, refer to the Basics chapter, on page 18.

MATERIALS & TOOLS

Canes or mokume gane veneer
   Round and hexagonal canes are the most appropriate shapes to cover the round cores in this tutorial.

Clay for the bead core
   This can be scrap clay or clay of a color that harmonizes with your patterns.

Skewer, small rod, or other tool

Small circle cutters (for mokume gane)

A small, clear acrylic sheet or the lid of a jar
   Any small flat smooth surface about 3 inches (8 cm) wide will work.

Latex gloves
   Wear as you shape and pierce the beads; this will avoid leaving fingerprints.

STEP BY STEP

1. Form a small ball of clay for the core of the bead. You can use scrap clay if you plan to completely cover the core, or you can use colored clay and leave the core visible.

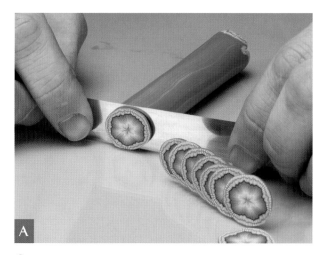

2. If you are using a cane to pattern the beads, make thin slices, about 1/16 inch (2 mm) (photo A). Remember that stiffer clay slices better. You can always cool your cane in the freezer for a bit if it is not slicing well. If you are using mokume gane, roll it out on a medium pasta machine setting. Use a circle cutter to cut out pieces of the mokume gane sheet to cover the bead core.

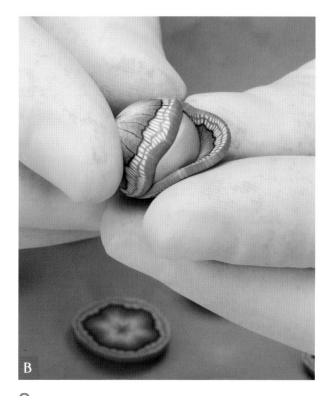

3. Place two patterned pieces on opposite sides of the ball of clay (photo B).

4. Experiment with sizing of the ball and slices. You can either bring the edges of your slices together and completely cover the inner ball, or leave it exposed.

5. Bring together the edges of the patterned slices and roll the clay into a ball between the palms of your hands. If you want a spherical (round) bead, all you need do is pierce it with a toothpick and bake. For other shapes, see the pages that follow.

VARIATIONS

C

D

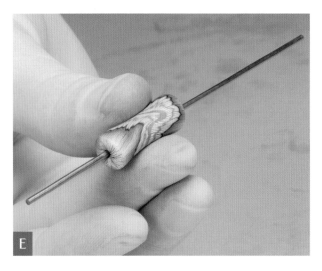

E

Tube beads: Roll the ball of clay on your work surface with your fingertips, pierce, and bake. If you prefer, roll the clay with the acrylic sheet (photos C and D). The advantage of the acrylic sheet is clear: You can see through it. For more of a bone shape, leave the bead on your skewer and roll the middle between your fingertips (photo E).

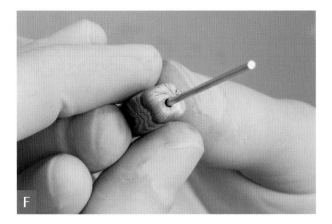

F

Baguette: Make a tube bead, pierce it, leave it on the skewer, and then pinch it between your fingers to create an elongated box form (photo F). You can square up the bead by pressing with the acrylic sheet on your work surface.

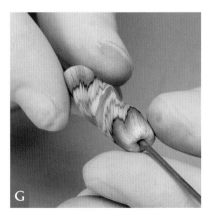

G

Spiral: Make a baguette shape and twist it on the skewer (photo G).

Teardrop: Proceed as in making a tube bead, but press more on one end of the tube (photo H).

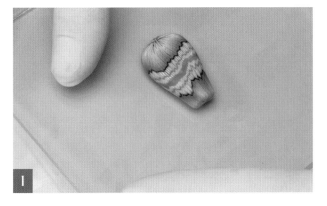

Flattened teardrop: Roll a teardrop shape and then flatten the large end against the work surface with the acrylic sheet (photo I). Pierce and bake.

Wedge: Pinch the ball of clay between your fingers (photo J). Pierce and bake.

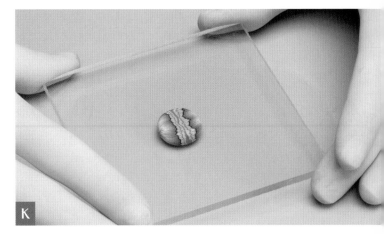

Disc: Flatten the sphere bead with the acrylic sheet (photo K).

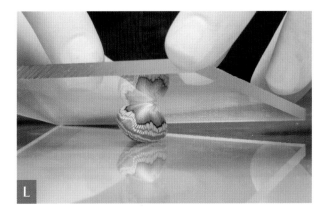

Bicone: Press the bead against your work surface with the clear acrylic sheet, and move your hand in small circles. Press lightly at first and then gradually increase the pressure. Hold the acrylic sheet parallel to your work surface, making a small cranking motion. The idea is to get the ball of clay to wobble on its axis. As it does, it will form a point against the table and a point against the acrylic sheet, connected by two beautifully coned surfaces (photo L).

PEARLIZED

MICA-CLAY BEADS

Mica is the magic in some pearlized polymer clays. This mica is synthetic and takes the form of small, glittery particles with reflective qualities that can be manipulated in different ways to create mysterious visual effects.

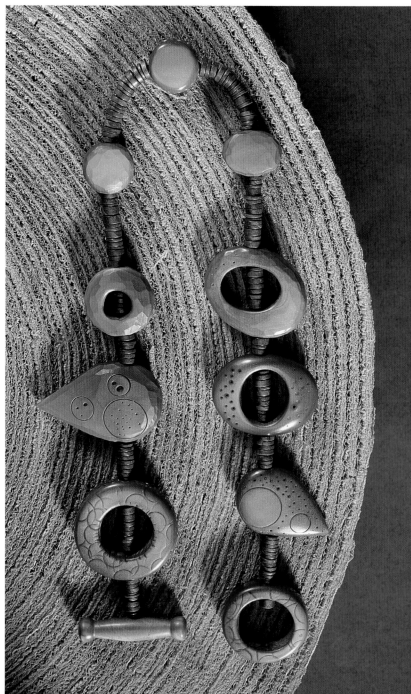

Grant Diffendaffer. *Necklace,* 2007. 22 inches (56 cm) long, largest bead 2 inches (5 cm) long. Polymer cookie-cutter beads (hand carved, textured, backfilled), polymer accent beads and lathe-turned toggle, buna cord.

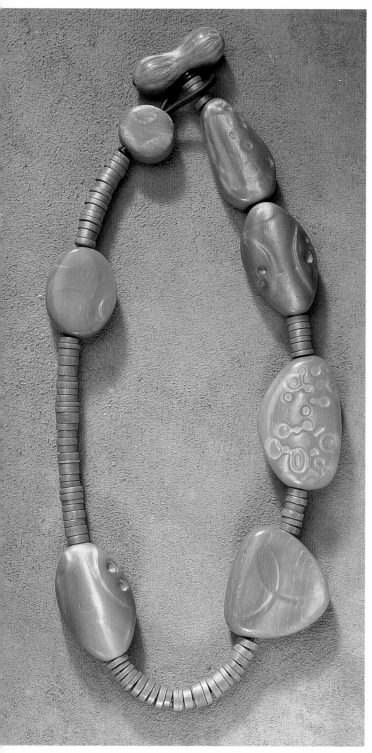

Grant Diffendaffer. *Necklace,* 2007. 21 inches (53 cm) long; largest bead 1¾ inches (4 cm) long. Polymer ghost-image beads, polymer accent beads and lathe-turned toggle, buna cord.

CLAY PREPARATION

Before you make beads with mica clay, you must first prepare the clay to achieve the proper results. After this introductory section, the bead tutorials begin on page 34.

So what is a mica-shift effect? Something more easily experienced than explained. By playing with the orientation of the particles within the clay, you can create a shifting variation of shade on the surface of the clay. In other words, using only one color of clay, you can create patterns of light that shift, depending on the angle from which you view them. These effects can create dramatic movement of light and illusions of depth on the surface of your beads. This is known as "chatoyance," a French word that means an effect "like a cat's eye." If you have ever seen a tiger's-eye or cat's-eye stone, you are familiar with the effect.

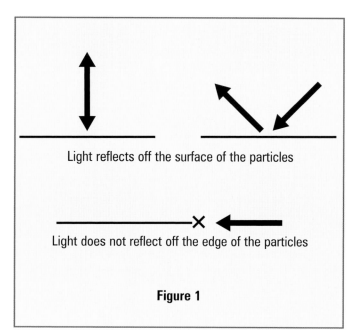

Light reflects off the surface of the particles

Light does not reflect off the edge of the particles

Figure 1

You can imagine the mica particles acting like little mirrors, with two shiny surfaces, back to back. Light bounces off the flat surface of the flakes just as it does off mirrors (figure 1).

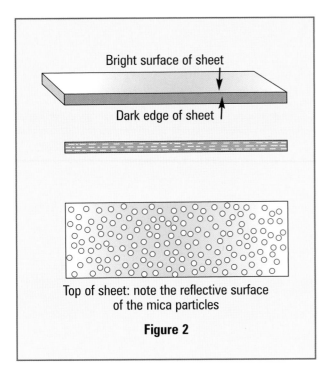

Bright surface of sheet

Dark edge of sheet

Top of sheet: note the reflective surface of the mica particles

Figure 2

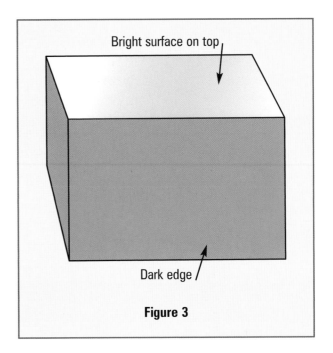

Bright surface on top

Dark edge

Figure 3

In pearlized polymer clay, the mica particles are scattered helter-skelter. Luckily for us, we can easily organize the particles by running the clay through the pasta machine. The resulting alignment takes about as long as it normally does to condition a sheet of clay. The result? The particles align themselves in the same direction, so that their reflective surfaces are parallel to the surface of the sheet of clay. Trim the edges and you will notice that the surface is brighter than the edges of the sheet (figure 2).

Note: Not all clays work for mica-shift techniques, and not all brands of pearlized polymer clay contain mica, so if you are not sure whether a clay is appropriate, ask where you buy your clay.

This is the foundation of all mica-shift techniques. After initially aligning the mica particles, there are numerous ways of realigning them to achieve different mica-shift effects.

The sheets of clay can be stacked into an organized block—what polymer pioneers Pier Voulkos and Mike Buesseler called an "ingot"—with a bright surface on the top and bottom and a dark surface along the edges (figure 3). The sheets can be rolled up into a spiral tube, or "jellyroll" ingot. These blocks and rolls can be cut apart and reassembled into new ingots, in the fashion of a cane. Instead of using different colors of clay, you create contrast through the varying mica orientations of adjacent sheets of clay. (The difference between a mica ingot and a cane: If you reduce a mica ingot as you reduce a cane, the mica particles will realign themselves with the side walls of the cane and you will lose contrast in the cross-sectional slices you make from the ends. Pier Voulkos discovered that by running these slices through the pasta machine, she could bring the patterns back out. She called this technique "invisible caning.")

The first three beads in this chapter were made from solid pieces of different ingots. The fourth, the veneered pillow bead, is made with a veneer, or thin sheet of patterned clay, which covers a core bead. Following are instructions for creating ingots.

INGOT VARIETIES

In a nutshell, making an ingot involves stacking sheets of conditioned mica clay into a block. You can make the ingot any size you want. I like to make big ones! Don't get hung up on measurements, as they will vary somewhat from one pasta machine to another.

Basic Ingots

1. Condition your clay. By the time you are finished, all mica particles will align with the surface of your sheet.

2. Roll out a 24-inch-long (31 cm) sheet.

3. Cut the sheet in half and stack one half on top of the other. Roll the sheets with a brayer or roller to seal them together (photo A).

4. Cut the double sheet in half, and stack one half on the other. Roll again with a brayer or roller. You now have a four-layer ingot.

5. Cut the four-layer ingot in half. Stack and roll again. The ingot is now eight layers thick, measures 3 inches (8 cm) wide, and is as long as your pasta machine is wide (mine is 5½ inches, or 14 cm).

6. Cut the ingot widthwise (perpendicular to your previous cuts). Stack and compress once more (photo B).

Realigned Ingots

1. Create a basic ingot measuring about 3 x 3 x 3 inches (8 cubic cm).

2. Turn the ingot on its side, so that a dark surface faces up.

3. Mark a square on the end of the ingot, with the corners of the square intersecting the middle of the sides of the original ingot (photo C).

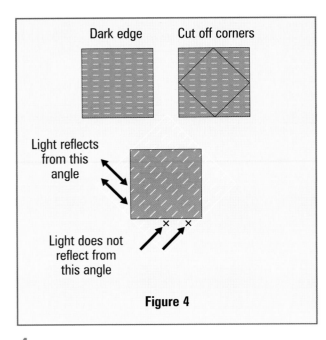

Figure 4

4. Cut off the corners of the original ingot. The resulting ingot, cut from the middle of the original, is realigned, with two dark surfaces and four surfaces that appear bright from one angle and dark from another (figure 4).

Jellyroll Ingots

This is one of my favorites. Play with its simple and dramatic effects and I'm sure you will agree.

1. Condition a 10-inch-long (25 cm) sheet of clay.

2. Roll up the sheet from one end to the other. Take care not to trap air as you roll. The result is essentially a one-color jelly roll cane.

3. Roll the jellyroll back and forth on your work surface. Apply pressure and lengthen the cane so that the layers seal together.

4. Slice off the ends of the cane (figure 5).

5. Cut the cane into approximately 3-inch (8 cm) segments.

6. Stand a cane segment on the flat cut-off end.

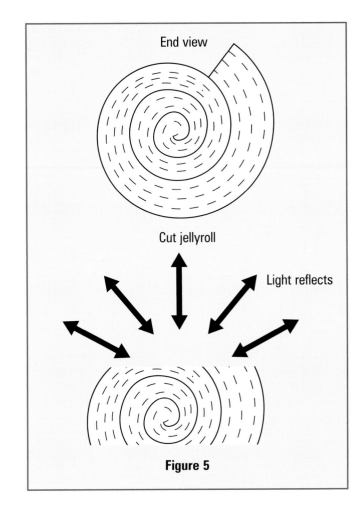

Figure 5

7. Remove two vertical slices of clay with your tissue blade. Cut off about one-quarter the width of the cane from the side facing you, and about one-quarter from the side facing away. This will leave the middle section intact (photo D).

Notice the mica-shift effect on the cut sides. The light plays off the flat surface as if it were the outside of a cylinder, shifting from side to side as you move the ingot. The slices you removed will display the opposite effect, with light playing off the flat surface as if it were the inside of a cylinder.

"Cane-Style" Ingots

Are these canes or are they ingots? The answer is both, sort of. Pearlized clay doesn't work for traditional canes, since the reduction process causes the mica particles to align their bright surfaces with the side, instead of the patterned end, of the cane. So you see only the dark version of the clay when you slice the cane. While you may like the resulting color, there will be no mica shift and less contrast. The solution is to make ingots, or canes that you don't reduce. Try these simple ones:

Striped Ingots

1. Create a 2½ x 2½-inch (6 square cm) ingot.

E

2. Place your ingot with one bright side on the top and one on the bottom. The other four sides should be dark. Slicing vertically through the ingot, remove slices measuring about ⅛ to ³⁄₁₆ inch (3 to 5 mm) thick (photo E).

F

3. After slicing up the ingot, re-stack the slices, rotating every other slice as you go, to create a striped ingot (photo F).

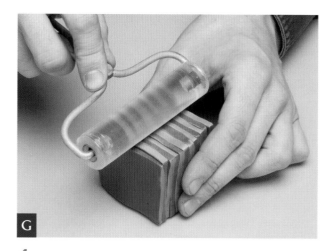

G

4. Compress the ingot with your fingers and press it against your work surface with a brayer to seal the slices together (photo G).

5. Trim the uneven edges with your tissue blade (photo H).

Ripple-Striped Ingots

1. Create a 2½ x 2½-inch (6 square cm) ingot.

2. Place your ingot with one bright side on the top, and one on the bottom. The four sides should be dark.

3. Using a ripple-striped blade, slice vertically through the ingot, making slices of about ⅛ to ³⁄₁₆ inch (3 to 5 mm) thick. Slice half of the ingot in this way (photo I).

4. Turn the ingot so that one of the dark sides faces up. Slice vertically into the ingot, making ⅛ to ³⁄₁₆-inch (3 to 5 mm) slices. Slice the remainder of the ingot in this fashion (photo J).

5. Recombine the ingot, alternating bright and dark slices. Take care to line up the waves in the slices so that you do not trap air (photo K).

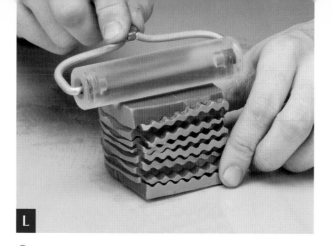

L

6. Compress the ingot with your fingers and press it against your work surface with a brayer to seal the slices together (photo L).

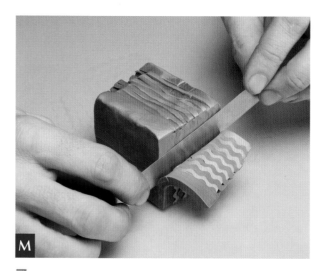

M

7. Trim the uneven edges with your tissue blade (photo M).

Ingot tips

In addition to deliberately assembling the clay body to display chatoyant effects and patterning, you can distort the clay body or surface to achieve other effects. Bending or twisting the entire ingot is an example of distorting the whole clay body. This will affect the organization of the interior, and the play of light on the surface of any slices you make.

Realigned Ripple-Striped Ingots

1. Create a realigned ingot measuring about 2½ inches (6 cm) on each side.

2. Place the ingot on your work surface with one dark side on the left and one on the right. The other four sides should look bright if viewed from the correct angle.

N

O

3. Using the ripple-striped blade, remove slices approximately ⅛ inch (3 mm) thick from either the side facing you or the side facing away, whichever is more comfortable for you. Lay the slices on your work surface just as they come off the ingot (photo N). Don't rotate or flip them. Slice up the whole ingot in this fashion and lay out the slices in rows. Then rotate every other slice by 180° (photo O).

4. Taking the slices in order from your work surface, reassemble the ingot. Take care not to leave any spaces between the slices.

5. Compress the ingot with your fingers and roll it with the brayer to seal the slices together.

Beads

The bead tutorials on the following pages focus on individual techniques. When you are comfortable with them, try combining techniques. Make carved cookie-cutter beads, cookie-cut ghost-image beads, ghost-image pillow beads, and so on.

BRUISING

If you press your thumb into an ingot and cut through the impression, the mica surrounding it will shift. This technique, known as "bruising," is visually impressive and very useful.

Here are five basic ways to do bruising. All work best with softer clay.

- Making dimples or small impressions in the surface of a bead. A ball stylus is perfect for this. When beads are sanded, they will be outlined with mica-shift effect.

- Making deep impressions in the ingot and then "healing" them (squeezing the clay together and sealing the cuts you have made). Note that you can't even cut into an ingot without having your blade leave a faint mark when the ingot is sealed back together. Cutting with the back of your blade, because it is not as sharp, and thus creates more drag as it moves through the clay, will yield a more dramatic effect—but don't cut yourself! Alternately, try cutting into the clay with the edge of a plastic card. The thicker the tool, the more drag, and so the more dramatic the bruising effect.

- Using the ghost-image effect (see page 52), a controlled way of bruising a large surface with a specific texture. When the texture is cut away, the resulting smooth surface will have an image of the original texture, which looks three-dimensional. Even though the surface of the clay is smooth, the light reflects as if it were textured.

- Backfilling texture. When you press a sheet of mica clay into the cured texture of a bead, the mica particles flow to follow the impressions. When you cut away the excess clay, you will have a smooth surface that behaves like a ghost image.

- Dragging the mica across the surface of the clay, which happens any time you cut through mica with your blade. You can do this in a painterly fashion when you carve beads, using a ball stylus or similar tool to "draw" on the surface of the raw clay. The effect will be most noticeable on surfaces with a "dark" orientation, where the dragged impression will show up as light.

You can layer the results of these five techniques atop one another for rich and varied surfaces.

COOKIE-CUTTER BEADS

These simple beads display the mica shift in all its glory and really offer you bang for the buck. In a medium that offers plenty of showy techniques, they stand out by showcasing the inherent beauty of pearlized clay.

TOOLS & MATERIALS

Clay cutters
Choose your desired size and shape.

An ingot
It should measure 3 inches (8 cm) long, as wide as your pasta machine, and ½ inch (1 cm) thick or slightly thinner (as thick as you want your beads to be). This technique works with any ingot, but is simple and impressive with a plain ingot.

STEP BY STEP

1. With a slice of an ingot slightly thicker than the desired thickness of the finished bead, cut out shapes with clay cutters or cookie cutters (photo A).

2. Remove the clay from the cutter and pierce with a needle, skewer, or toothpick to form a bead.

3. Cure the bead, sand, and buff it to finish.

VARIATIONS

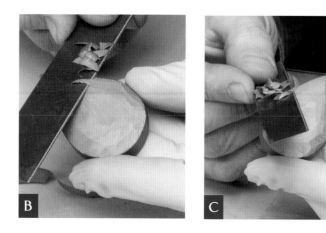

1. Carve and facet the beads with your tissue blade (photos B and C). For more on this technique, see page 51.

2. Try using a patterned slice of a mokume gane brick instead of a mica ingot.

3. Stretch and hand-mold the beads into various forms. (Use latex gloves to avoid interfering with the mica on the surface of the clay. You will likely have to sand into such a bead to remove the surface mica and reveal the more impressive mica shift within.)

4. Make impressions in the raw clay with a ball stylus or other tool. Bake the bead and "backfill" the impressions with raw clay in contrasting colors. Bake again and finish (photo D).

CARVED-INGOT BEADS

This technique takes advantage of the simple beauty of the mica shift. No fancy patterns here, just sumptuous curves, striking facets, and the soft shimmer of the mica shift. This bead is effective with any ingot style. Start with a plain ingot, then a ripple-striped one, then a plain one bruised with your blade.

TOOLS & MATERIALS

A striped ingot
A tissue blade and a mandrel
A latex glove

STEP BY STEP

1. Cut a piece of striped ingot measuring ¾ x ¾ x 2 inches (2 x 2 x 5 cm).

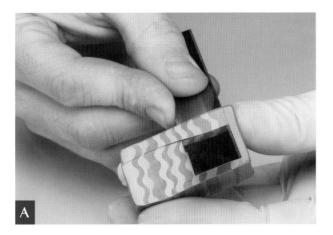

2. Using your tissue blade, slice off the edges and corners of the ingot, cutting about ¼ inch (6 mm) into the ingot each time (photo A). Wearing a latex glove on the hand holding the bead will protect its surface from fingerprints.

3. Continue carving the ingot in this fashion, gradually shaping it into a bead. With each slice, add another faceted surface to the bead.

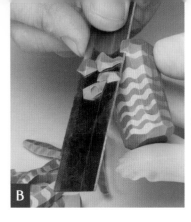

4. After you have roughed out a bead form, continue carving it, making smaller and smaller slices to refine the shape (photo B).

5. Pierce and bake the bead. The faceted finish can be beautiful as is, but if you wish, you can sand the bead smooth and buff it. Faceting is great for simpler ingots, but more complex surface patterns are better revealed if you sand away the top layer of clay which, after all the manipulation, is usually covered with randomly oriented mica particles. The resulting finish will have much more depth and luminosity.

VARIATIONS

Try making impressions in the raw clay with a ball stylus or other tool. Bake the bead and backfill the impressions with raw clay in contrasting colors. Bake again and finish. Hand-form the beads after you have carved them. Wear latex gloves to minimize interference with mica on the surface of the clay. Roll the beads between your palms to smooth the surfaces and then form them with your fingertips. You can create smooth and lustrous beads this way with a minimum of finishing (photo C).

GHOST-IMAGE BEADS

Ghost imaging is a technique whereby an illusion of three-dimensional texture is created on a smooth surface. Ghost imaging involves stamping a texture into the clay and cutting it away with a blade. The surface can then either be rolled smooth and used as a veneer, or cured and sanded smooth.

When the texture plate is pressed into the clay, the clay flows to fill the texture and the mica realigns. In the floors of the texture, parallel to the original surface of the clay, the mica retains its original orientation. As the clay transitions from the floor to the walls of the texture, the mica particles bend to follow the new surface. As the texture peaks, the particles again bend to follow the top surface of the clay. All of this re-orientation sinks into the clay. When you cut the texture away, the mica particles below retain that orientation and cause light to play off the smooth surface as if it were still textured.

The ghost-image effect can be varied in a number of ways. You can simply imprint a texture into a conditioned sheet of clay and cut, or you can stack or roll up the sheet and stamp the resulting ingot. You can use just one color of clay, or you can use layers or blends of clay.

This tutorial involves using a realigned ingot from a single color. The effect causes the ghost image to look bright from one angle and dark from another.

TOOLS & MATERIALS

A "realigned" ingot
An ingot measuring about 3 inches (8 cm) on each side is large enough to make six or more beads.

Texture sheets with bold, deep textures

Two ½-inch-thick (1 cm) spacers
You can make these from a piece of wood or scrap clay. Spacers should measure about 6 inches (15 cm) long by ½ inch (1 cm) thick by ½ inch (1 cm) wide.

A spray bottle filled with water

STEP BY STEP

1. Place the ingot on your work surface with a dark surface up and a dark surface down. Each of the other four sides should look bright, viewed from the correct angle.

2. Slice vertically down into the dark end of the ingot, removing a piece measuring approximately ¾ inch (2 cm) thick.

3. Choose two texture sheets and spray them liberally with water.

4. Place the ingot slice on top of one of the sheets.

5. Place two spacers about ½ inch (1 cm) thick on opposite sides of the ingot slice (photo A).

6. Place the other texture sheet on top of the ingot slice and press down on it with a board or hardback book. The ingot will compress until the spacers stop it.

7. Remove the ingot from between the texture sheets, taking care not to distort or stretch it.

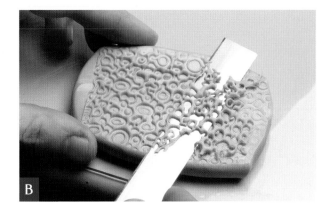

8. Place the ingot at the edge of your work surface. Holding a tissue blade in one hand and securing the ingot with the other, slice away the texture. Take care to remove the bumps but not to cut below the impressions. As you will be sanding the bead after curing it, you need not create a perfectly smooth surface now (photo B).

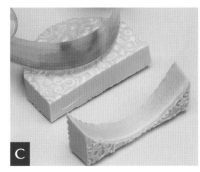

9. Cut the ingot slice into the desired shape. I like to bend my blade and make curved cuts (photo C).

10. Pierce the bead with a skewer and cure it.

11. Sand and buff the bead to finish it.

VENEERED PILLOW BEADS

Working with mica veneers can be tricky. Too much handling can distort the effects that make this clay so special. In the last tutorial, I described how you can make a bead from a solid block of clay, or ingot. One of the advantages of working with an ingot in this way: You can minimize the handling of the patterned clay in its raw state by smoothing and shaping it after it is cured.

Veneered pillow beads let you make the most of both the raw and cured properties of polymer clay by using a multi-stage assembly-and-curing process. Start by making a core bead that you cure in the oven and then cover with patterned veneers (sheets) of clay. By patterning and curing the bead one side at a time, you can avoid damaging one surface as you work on another. I found the pattern in this tutorial as I sliced into a ripple-striped ingot to add another stripe from a perpendicular angle. I had planned to carve the ingot into a bead, but what I saw inside gave me new ideas. The effect is other-worldly and beguiling.

TOOLS & MATERIALS

A 2 x 2-inch (8 square cm) ripple-striped ingot
A ripple blade
¹⁄₁₆-inch mandrel (or similar slender skewer)
A hobby knife

STEP BY STEP

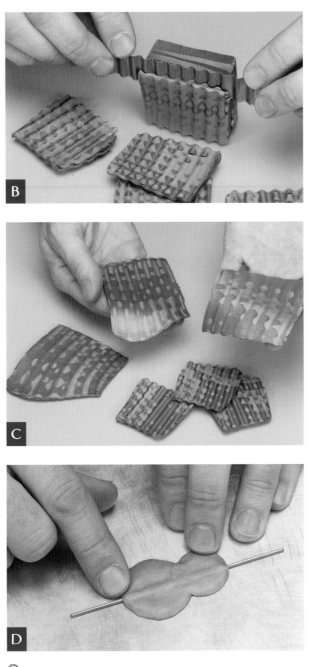

1. Slice up your ingot to create veneers. Place a realigned ripple-striped ingot on your work surface, oriented so that the ripple stripes are visible on the left and right sides. The stripes should be vertical, beginning from the work surface and pointing up (photo A).

2. Using your ripple blade, slice down into the ingot (photo B), removing slices about ⅛ inch (3 mm) thick or slightly thicker. You should notice a pattern on the rippled surface where the blade cuts through more than one stripe at a time. Roll these slices out to a medium thickness on your pasta machine and set aside (photo C).

3. Place a bead mandrel or skewer on your baking sheet and build a thin shape around it with scrap clay. Cover the mandrel smoothly with clay, and taper the shape around the edges towards the baking sheet. Cure in the oven for 20 minutes (photo D).

4. Smear a thin layer of raw clay on the core bead (photo E).

5. Lay the patterned veneer over the bead.

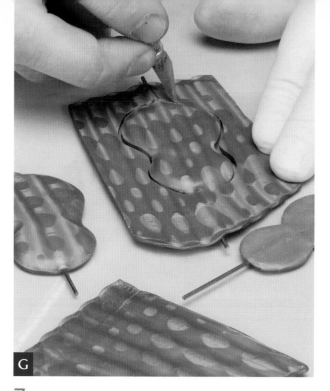

7. Use a pointy-blade hobby knife to cut out the shape of the bead (photo G).

8. Bake.

9. Remove the bead from the baking tray and smear raw clay onto the back.

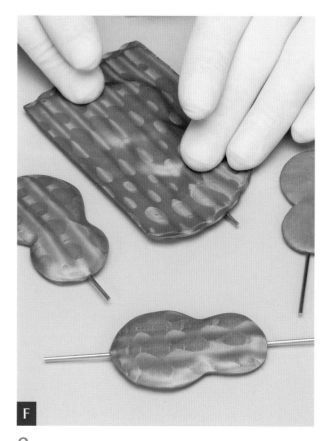

6. Press the veneer gently but firmly into place over the core bead (photo F).

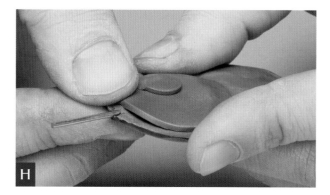

10. Use scrap clay to build out the form of the bead from the nonpatterned back (photo H).

11. Bake.

12. Smear raw clay onto the nonpatterned side of the bead.

13. Gently but firmly adhere the patterned veneer to the bead and trim the edges with your hobby knife. Pinch and stroke the edges of the raw clay to create a clean seam around the edge of the bead (photos I and J).

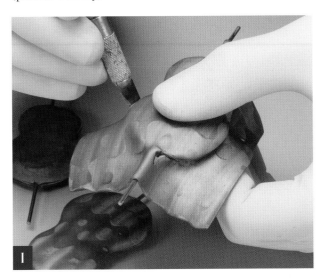

14. Bake.

15. Sand and buff to finish.

VARIATION

These beads can be made with any kind of patterned veneer. Try ghost-image veneers, made by impressing a texture into a sheet of clay, cutting away the texture, and rolling the clay smooth in the pasta machine. You can also use caned veneers or mokume gane.

Grant Diffendaffer and **Kirsten Anderson.** *Necklace,* 2007. 19 inches (48 cm) long; beads 2 ¼ x 1½ inches (6 x 4 cm). Polymer pillow beads with pearlized clay veneer, polymer accent beads and toggle, black onyx, nylon-coated stainless steel wire, buna cord.

TEXTURED
BEADS

I love organic patterns. Mysterious, flowing, and ever-varied, organically patterned beads seem to have sprung fully formed right from nature. I could have created such beads by sculpting them individually. But I wanted a way to quickly and easily create symmetrical multiples. Using a stamp or texture mold presented difficulties: Pressing raw clay against a flat texture sheet distorts the bead form without even providing a deep impression. Texturing a sheet of clay and then wrapping it around a core would mean having to hide a seam. I also worried about distorting the pattern and leaving unsightly fingerprints. Eventually I developed two different methods of creating textured beads that I share with you here.

Grant Diffendaffer. *Necklace,* 2007. 84 inches (213 cm) long; beads 2 inches (5 cm) long. Polymer textured tube beads, polymer accent beads, buna cord.

TEXTURED TUBE BEADS

To create the first set of beads, I put a cured core bead on a mandrel and covered it with a thin layer of raw clay. This allowed me to roll the bead across the texture sheet without distorting the form or touching the raw clay with my hands. The result was a slender tube bead with lush, interlocking texture.

TOOLS & MATERIALS

Tube beads

Use these as bead cores (see the Basics chapter, page 27). I assume you know all about these.

Polymer clay in your choice of color

I prefer pearlized clays because of the mica-shift effect. Choose one color for the raised portions of the bead and one color for the impressed texture. It takes just a little bit of each to make a bead.

⅛-inch (3 mm) bead mandrels

Polymer clay or RTV silicone texture sheets

Ideal texture sheets will be densely patterned with textures about ¹⁄₁₆-inch (2 mm) deep. (See the Basics chapter, page 24.)

Spray bottle of water

Dome molds for shaping the ends of the beads (see below).

Wet/dry sandpaper in the following grits: 220, 320, 400, 600, 800, 1000, and 1200.

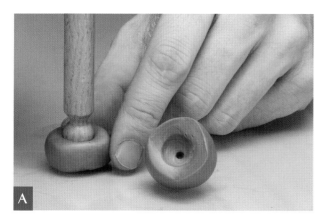

BEFORE YOU BEGIN

(To make a dome mold, find a domed shape slightly larger than the end of your bead. Try pressing the end of a tool handle, a marble, or a dapping tool into a small lump of clay and poke a hole through the middle of the impression with a ⅛-inch (3 mm) mandrel. Wiggle the mandrel a bit to stretch the hole. (If you skip this last step, the hole will shrink in the oven and your mandrel will no longer fit through.) Create two end molds (photo A) and cure them in the oven.

STEP BY STEP

1. Center a tube bead on a 6-inch (15 cm) mandrel. The bead should be about ¼ to ⅜ inch (6 to 10 mm) in diameter. If you didn't texturize the bead before baking, scrape it up with some low-grit sandpaper.

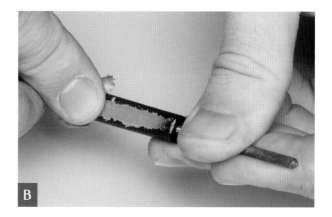

2. Decide on the color for your finished bead, and smear a thin layer of clay into the sandpapered texture on the bead to ensure that the clay will stick (photo B).

3. Layer the core with enough clay to fill the texture on your texture sheet, but not so much that the bead shape is greatly distorted when you roll it. This works out to a medium setting on my machine.

4. Prepare the clay to cover the bead with. Choose a color for the raised portions of the texture and roll out a 3-inch (8 cm) sheet on your thickest pasta-machine setting. Roll out a 3-inch (8 cm) sheet of the other color on your thinnest setting. Layer these two sheets together and run them through on a medium setting (photo C).

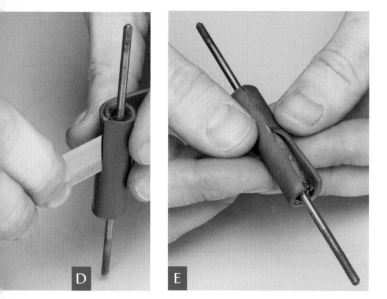

D

E

F

5. Cut a strip of the layered clay about ⅛ inch (3 mm) longer than the core bead, and lay it on your work surface, thin layer down. Lay the bead across it so that it overlaps by 1/16 inch (2 mm) on each end. Wrap the clay once around the core bead, and trim it where it overlaps (photo D). Butt the ends together and try to hide the bottom layer of clay at the seams by making a clean joint. Roll the bead on your work surface, pressing the clay with your fingers to seal the seam and make the clay adhere to the core bead. Wrap the clay around the ends to cover the core up to the mandrel (photo E). Use a needle tool to pop any air bubbles.

6. Thoroughly spray the texture sheet with water to act as a release. (RTV silicone sheets will not require any release.) Note: Some clays become gummy as they come into contact with water. If you have this problem, use cornstarch as a release. Take care to keep the cornstarch out of your raw clay supply, as it will weaken it.

7. Place the bead on the texture sheet and gently but firmly press on the mandrel to impart texture to the bead. Lightly rocking the bead from one end to the other will help ensure that it is fully and deeply textured (photo F).

8. Release pressure and roll the bead slightly forward without lifting it from the texture sheet. Repeat the pressing process. Continue until the whole bead is textured, overlapping the texture slightly at the end.

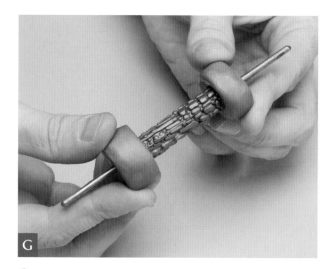

G

9. Spray the domed end molds with water and slide them onto the ends of your bead mandrel, pressing the bead between them (photo G).

10. Use your ball stylus, sandpaper, or needle tool to further sculpt and texture your bead. This is a great way to quickly and easily add variation to beads.

11. Bake the bead to the clay manufacturer's recommended specifications.

12. Sand and buff to finish. If you are sanding by hand, I suggest starting with 400-grit. If sanding on a lathe, begin with 220. (The lathe is efficient at getting out the scratches from the lower grits, which can be difficult to do by hand.) Sand with the initial grit until the second layer of clay is revealed and the bead is shaped to your satisfaction.

VARIATIONS

A simpler version of this bead: Create contrast between the raised and etched portions of the design by antiquing the bead with acrylic paint. Cover the bead with paint and wipe off the excess, leaving paint in the crevices and highlighting the texture. It is easier to control the contrast of the paint with the clay than with clay alone. You may enjoy applying several layers of paints for varied effects. The disadvantages to the acrylic paint method are the extra steps to finish the bead, the mess, and the fact that the color is not an integral part of the bead.

To antique a bead, coat the whole bead with acrylic paint in a contrasting color. Wipe off the excess with a paper towel. Bake the bead again at 250°F (121°C) for 20 minutes to dry and bond the paint.

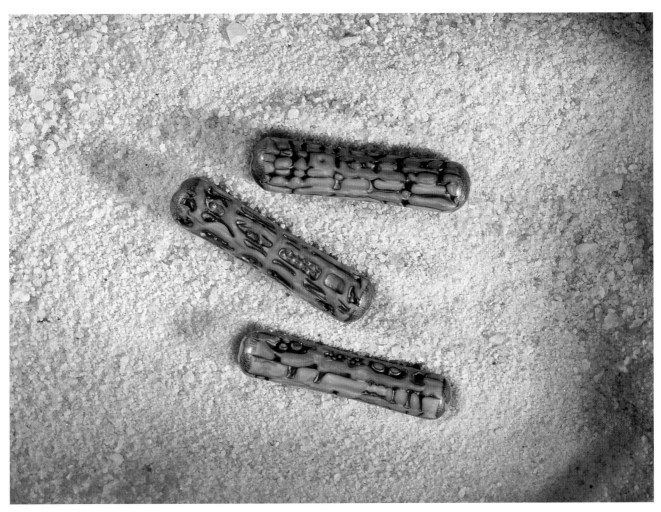

TEXTURED DISCS AND SPHERES

Textured discs and spheres take the texturing process to the next level—essentially the same process as the tube beads, but rather than layering raw clay over a baked tube, you layer it over a rounded form. You'll need to make a curved texture plate, or texture channel. This is a bit tricky and time-consuming, but the rewards are well worth it.

TOOLS & MATERIALS

Tube beads (see Basics chapter, page 27)
⅛-inch (3 mm) bead mandrels (see Basics chapter, page 28)
8-inch (20 cm) sheet of scrap clay
  Use this to create a texture channel.
Texture tools, such as ball stylus and sharp pebbles
Spray bottle of water
Polymer clay in your choice of color
  I prefer pearlized clays for their mica-shift effect.
A wooden dowel, 8 inches (20 cm) long and ¼ inch to 1 inch (1 to 3 cm) in diameter
  The larger the dowel, the larger the bead.
Wet/dry sandpaper in the following grits: 220, 320, 400, 600, 800, 1000, and 1200

STEP BY STEP

1. To create the texture channel, condition your scrap clay so that it is soft—the softer, the better.

2. Roll your sheet of scrap clay into a tube.

3. Lay your dowel lengthwise on top of the tube of clay (photo A).

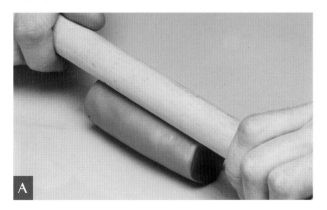

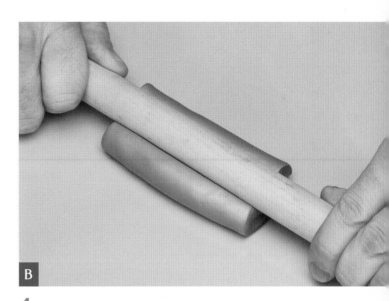

4. Press down on the dowel so that it sinks into the clay halfway up the diameter of the dowel. Do not press more than halfway because you will be texturing the sides of the channel, which will in turn be used to texture your bead (photo B).

5. The height of the clay will vary somewhat along the length of the dowel. Using a board, hardback book, or a similarly rigid, flat surface, press the clay to create an even surface (photo C).

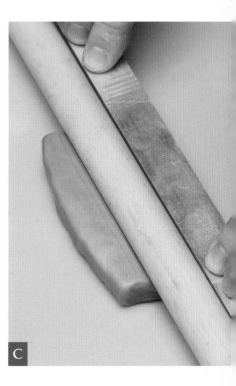

D

6. Remove the dowel. You should have a smooth channel with walls of equal height on each side (photo D).

E

7. Texture the channel with your texture tools. Press straight down towards your work surface. Make the texture densely detailed. Spending time on your texture channel will really pay off (photo E).

8. Cure the channel in the oven to the clay manufacturer's specifications.

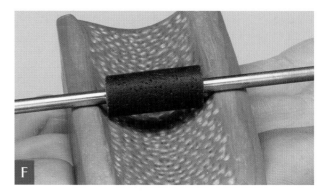

F

9. To create a core bead, build up layers of raw clay on a cured tube bead, until the bead fits the channel. Using a tissue blade, cut the tube bead short enough so that when you put it on a mandrel and lay the mandrel across the channel, the bead fits entirely inside the channel. The length of the tube bead will vary depending on the width of the channel and the thickness of the original bead (photo F).

10. If you didn't texturize your tube bead before baking, scrape it up with low-grit sandpaper.

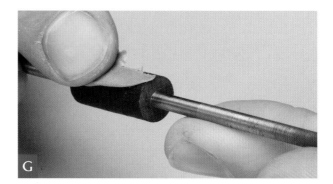

G

11. Smear the tube bead with a thin layer of raw clay, as an adhesive for the next layer of clay (photo G).

12. Build up a core bead that perfectly fits the channel by rolling a sheet of clay (the color of your finished bead) on your thickest setting.

13. Cut a strip of clay about ⅛ inch (3 mm) wider than your tube bead and long enough to wrap around it.

H

14. Lay your bead on the strip of clay so the clay overlaps by about 1/16 inch (2 mm) on either end of the bead (photo H).

15. Wrap the clay around the bead once and trim off the excess. Press the clay onto the bead.

16. Roll the bead against your work surface, pressing it with your fingers so that the raw clay adheres securely to the core bead.

17. Spray the texture channel with water.

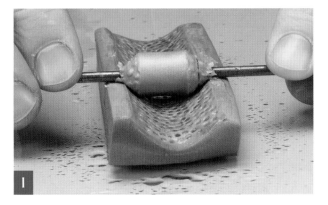

I

18. Place the bead in the texture channel. For a small bead (a quarter-dowel), the raw clay should make contact with the channel. For larger beads, the raw clay should connect with the channel at least on the ends of the bead. Roll the bead gently back and forth to shape the raw clay to the channel (photo I).

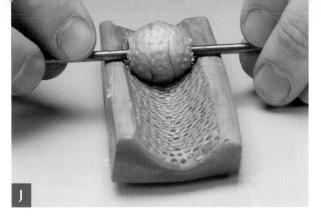

J

19. Larger beads will need multiple layers of clay to build the bead to sufficient size. Cut the second strip slightly narrower, and succeeding strips narrower still, so that the core bead approximates the shape of the channel. When there is enough clay on the core to make contact with the channel, roll it gently in the channel to round out the bead. With the ideal core bead, the mandrel will rest on the edges of the channel with the core bead against the inner surface (photo J).

20. Roll your core bead the length of the channel. Any low spots on the bead won't make contact with the channel. Add more clay to the bead in these spots.

21. Cure your bead in the oven, per the clay manufacturer's instructions.

22. After the bead is cured, rough it up with low-grit sandpaper.

23. Smear the surface of the bead with a thin layer of clay.

24. Prepare the clay to cover the bead. Choose a color for the raised portions of the texture, and roll out a 3-inch (8 cm) sheet on your thickest pasta machine setting. Roll out a 3-inch (8 cm) sheet of the other color on your thinnest pasta machine setting. Layer these two sheets together and run them through your pasta machine on a medium setting. You may need to experiment. If the clay is too thick, your bead will distort and you will not get a deep impression. If it is too thin, you will not get a deep impression either.

Grant Diffendaffer. *Necklace,* 2007. 19 inches (48 cm) long; beads 1½ inches (4 cm) long. Polymer textured beads, polymer accent beads and lathe-turned toggle, buna cord.

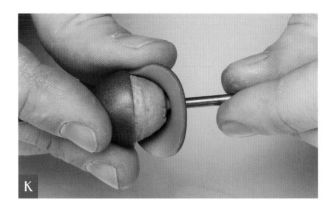

K

25. Cover the bead with the layered clay, applying the thick layer against the bead and the thin layer on top. Use a circle cutter to cut a circle large enough to cover half the bead, pierce it with the mandrel, slide it on, and wrap it over the bead. Do the same on the other side of the bead, and make the seam match up as well as possible to hide the bottom layer of clay. Press the clay firmly into place and pop any air bubbles with a needle tool (photo K).

L

26. Spray the texture channel thoroughly with water.

27. Place the bead in the channel and press down firmly on the mandrel, rocking it lightly from side to side (photo L).

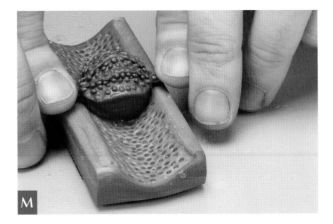

28. Lift up slightly on the mandrel and roll the bead lightly along the channel (photo M).

29. Press down firmly again and repeat the rocking motion.

30. Repeat steps 28 and 29 until the whole bead is textured.

31. If desired, embellish the bead using your texture tools. I find the ends of the beads often need some attention. A ball stylus can be used to make round impressions and to stretch out these impressions in a sculptural fashion. Sometimes I texture the ends lightly with sandpaper.

32. Finish the ends of the bead by pressing the clay into place with a rubber clay shaper (photo N).

33. Cure the bead for 30 minutes, at the manufacturer's recommended temperature.

34. Sand and buff to finish. If you are sanding by hand, start with the 400-grit. On a lathe, begin with the 220-grit. The lathe is efficient at getting out scratches from the lower grits, which can be very difficult to do by hand. Sand with the initial grit until the top layer of clay has been removed from the high points of texture. Continue sanding as much as you like, to shape the bead.

VARIATIONS

As with the tube bead, you can choose to antique this bead for contrast rather than using two contrasting colors of clay.

- For larger texture channels, try wrapping the dowel with twine or string when you make the original impression in your scrap clay (see step 4). This will create raised lines on your beads.

- If you leave untextured space when you bake your texture channel, you can carve it with a linoleum-carving tool later. I use a small V-gouge. Carving works better with larger channels.

- Try using flexible RTV silicone texture sheets with a blank channel. Place the texture sheet in the channel and roll your beads on it. One channel will yield a variety of textures.

- To bring in more color, try back-filling: Make impressions with your stylus (or other tool) in the raw clay of your bead. Cure it and then fill these impressions with colored clay.

LATHE-TURNED BEADS

Grant Diffendaffer. *Necklace,* 2007. 18½ inches (47 cm) long; largest bead 1½ (4 cm) inches long. Polymer beads (extruded, twisted, carved, antiqued, and lathe-turned); polymer spiny textured discs, polymer accent beads and toggle.

In nature, symmetry means life. It represents organization in a world of chaos. It implies direction and movement. I discovered that using a lathe enables me to easily make symmetrical beads that reflect my interest in the natural world. Seedpods, sea life, and microscopic organisms are some of my greatest influences, and so it's only natural that I would gravitate to this technique. However you color and pattern these beads, you will find that they look beautiful and feel amazing. Their varied surfaces invite tactile exploration.

I started out turning polymer clay with a drill press. Having worked with ceramics, it was natural for me to form the raw clay as it spun on the lathe. I achieved some success, but ultimately it was another ceramic technique that really represented a breakthrough—removing the raw clay using ceramic trimming tools.

The following tutorials are progressively more complex, ranging from turning raw clay to integrating metal end caps fastened with a tube rivet.

RAW-CLAY BEADS

Here is the most basic method of creating beads using a lathe: turning raw clay.

TOOLS & MATERIALS

All of the beads in this chapter require these basic tools and materials. Additional items are listed with each tutorial.

⅛-inch (3 mm) mandrels, approximately 6 inches (31 cm) long

These should be rubberized per instructions in the Basics chapter (page 28).

A lathe

For more on lathes, see the Basics chapter, under "Tools" (page 15).

Ceramic trimming tools

Small circle tools are the best, approximately ¼ inch (6 mm) in diameter or smaller. Buy the best and sharpest (probably the most expensive) ones you can find. They need to have a sharpened edge; a plain wire trimming tool will not work.

Safety goggles

Sandpaper, if you wish to sand and buff your beads

ADDITIONAL MATERIALS

Tube bead core, at least one, 1 to 2 inches (3 to 5 cm) long

Clay in your favorite color

I prefer pearlized clays because of the mica-shift effect, though nonpearlized clays work too. Clays of an overly soft or sticky consistency are poorly suited for lathe turning and will likely clog your tools. You will need sheets approximately 12 inches (31 cm) long, rolled on your thickest pasta machine setting, and as wide as your core bead, to make a 1-inch-diameter (3 cm) bead.

STEP BY STEP

1. Mount your tube bead on the rubberized mandrel (see Basics chapter, page 28).

2. If you did not texture your tube bead with sandpaper before baking, scrape it up with some sandpaper now.

3. Rub a thin layer of raw clay onto the surface of the bead to act as an adhesive for the raw clay that will be layered over it (photo A).

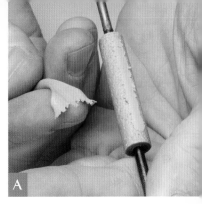

4. Roll out a sheet of clay on the thickest setting of your pasta machine. A 12-inch-long (31 cm) sheet is sufficient to make a bead approximately 1 inch (3 cm) in diameter. Cut it to about ¼ inch (6 mm) wider than your core bead, and set aside the rest.

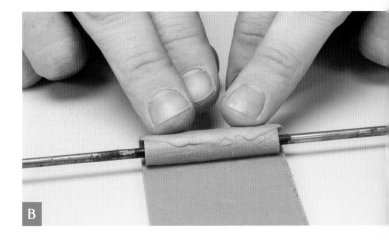

5. Place the core bead at one end of the sheet. Roll up the end halfway around the core, and press the clay firmly against the bead (photo B). Continue rolling, using sufficient pressure for the first layer of clay to bond with the core bead. Roll up the whole sheet, using pressure, to make sure the layers bond together, but don't press so hard that you make impressions in the clay as you roll, or you will likely end up with air bubbles, or gaps, between the layers, which can lead to cracks in your finished bead.

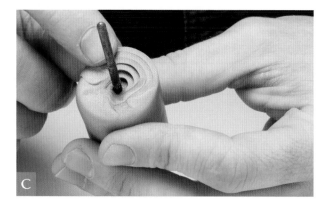

6. After rolling up the whole sheet, roll the tube of clay back and forth with your palm, compressing it, but not extending or distorting it. Pinch the ends down towards the mandrel a bit to seal the tube (photo C).

7. Place the mandrel in your lathe, which should be set up with a rotating chuck on the tailstock and a chuck on the headstock that will also hold the mandrel (photo D). Make sure that the lathe is set up to turn backwards. This will probably mean turning your lathe around, so that the top of the clay will turn away from you when you turn on the lathe.

8. Put on safety goggles.

9. Turn on your lathe at low speed. Experiment to determine the best speed. My lathe is a makeshift one, driven by a flex-shaft tool; I operate it at just above the very bottom range of its speed. If you turn the lathe too slowly, you will have difficulty accurately removing material. If you turn it too fast, the raw clay is likely to separate from the cured core bead and may even go flying off the lathe.

10. Lathes typically have a tool rest on them. I brace my left hand against the lathe and my work surface and, holding the tool in my right hand, steady it with my left thumb. The action is somewhat like holding a pool cue. Hold the trimming tool at about a 45° angle to the work surface (cutting end up), and use it to cut sideways into the turning clay where it meets the mandrel. (Either end is fine.) The clay should come off in a streamer or in small bits. Moving the tool away from the mandrel, flatten out the end of the clay roll (photo E).

11. As you come to the end of the clay, tip your cutting tool, make a smooth transition over the corner, and cut along the surface of the roll towards the other end. Your tool should meet the clay halfway between the top and side of the roll (photo F). You may notice a lot of vibration as the clay spins if your roll is off center. If you look closely, you will see that the profile of the spinning clay is defined by an inner line and an outer line—the difference

between the high and low points on the clay. If you remove the high points, the blur will become a nice, crisp line, the vibration should disappear, and you will have perfectly centered clay. You are well on your way to a symmetrical bead!

12. After you have smoothed out the surface of the clay, flatten out the uncut end, just as you did with the other.

13. Moving up the ends of the clay with your tool, roll it over onto the surface, rounding out the edges (photo G).

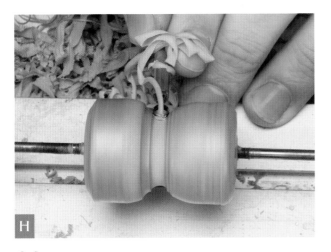

14. Work creatively with the clay: Round out the ends as much as you like. Cut the bead to any shape that pleases you. You can make one big round bead, cut it into multiple disc beads, or create any variety of curves along the profile of the bead. To make multiple beads from this one roll of clay, cut

down into the raw clay to define the individual beads, and stop when your trimming tool reaches the cured core. You can cut the beads apart after you have cured them (photo H).

15. Cure the beads in the oven, per the clay manufacturer's instructions. Let them cool in the oven to help prevent cracking.

16. Sand and buff the beads if you wish, or leave them as they are, or texturize them. Turning is a great technique to create core beads for your texture channels (see the Textured Discs and Spheres tutorial, on page 65). For texturizing complex forms, see the tutorial on page 83.

17. To remove the cured bead from the mandrel, put it back in the lathe. With the lathe holding the mandrel steady, you should be able to twist and push the bead free.

Tips

If your tool becomes gummed up with the raw clay, there are three ways to deal with this:

- Stop and clean out your trimming tool with a needle tool.

- Because warm clay presents more of a problem, try soaking your prepared clay and mandrel in an ice-water bath. (Note: some clays are water soluble and will get even gooier with water.)

- Try using firmer clay, perhaps of another brand.

CURED-CLAY BEADS

This is a great way to refine the shape of raw beads that you have turned and to take millefiori canework beads to another level. If you have been impressed by the symmetries in the patterned ends of your canes, just wait till you see what has been hiding within the sides!

TOOLS & MATERIALS

All of the beads in this chapter require these basic tools and materials. Additional items are listed with each tutorial.

⅛-inch (3 mm) mandrels, approximately 6 inches (31 cm) long

These should be rubberized, per instructions in the Basics chapter (page 28).

A lathe

For more on lathes, see the Basics chapter, under "Tools" (page 15).

Ceramic trimming tools

Small circle tools are the best, approximately ¼ inch (6 mm) in diameter or smaller. Buy the best and sharpest (probably the most expensive) ones you can find. They need to have a sharpened edge; a plain wire trimming tool will not work.

Safety goggles

Sandpaper, if you wish to sand and buff your beads

ADDITIONAL MATERIALS

A cured piece of clay

This can be a bead such as that created in the previous tutorial, a textured bead, or a cured piece of clay of any other sort, such as a cane. If you've cured a cane or other clay for this purpose, trim it with your tissue blade into a roughly cylindrical shape and then pierce it from one end to the other with a mandrel. Bake it on the mandrel.

STEP BY STEP

1. Affix your clay to a rubberized mandrel. (See Basics chapter, page 28.)

2. Place the mandrel in your lathe, set up with a rotating chuck on the tailstock and a chuck on the headstock. Make sure the lathe is set up to turn backwards. This will probably mean turning your lathe around so that the top of the clay turns away from you when you turn the lathe on.

3. Put on your safety goggles! A dust mask is a good idea too.

4. Turn the bead and cut it into the shape you want. Turning a bead that you formed on the lathe while raw is generally a matter of refining the existing shape. The process works exactly like turning raw clay. When the bead reaches the shape you desire, sand and buff it, or add clay and texturize it, as described in the tutorial on page 83. To turn a cane, or another irregularly shaped piece of clay, you need to center it by evening out the ends and then the top surface of the clay. With the high points cut off and the weight evenly centered on the mandrel, the turning process is much more manageable. Cut into the end where the clay meets the mandrel and move upwards, away from the mandrel, forming a smooth, flat surface (photo A).

5. Turn your tool and round the corner from the side to the top surface of the clay. Hold the tool at about a 45° angle to your work surface and cut down into the clay about halfway between the top and the side (photo B).

6. Stop the lathe periodically to see how far you have cut. To achieve uniform thickness, cut directly down towards the mandrel, at least as far as the lowest point within the path of your tool. When you have removed the high points to leave a centered surface, angle your cutting edge slightly and begin to move your tool towards the other end of the mandrel (photo C).

7. After you have removed all of the low points, flatten out the uncut end of your clay and cut it into whatever shape you want (photo D).

8. When you finish shaping your bead, sand and buff it.

Grant Diffendaffer and **Kirsten Anderson.**
Necklace, 2007. 19 inches (48 cm) long; largest bead 1½ inches (4 cm) long. Polymer lathe-turned millefiori beads, polymer clay accent beads and lathe-turned toggle, glass seed beads, multi-strand nylon-coated stainless steel wire.

EXTRUDED BEADS

I recently acquired an excellent extruder made specifically for polymer clay. Out of the many shapes it creates, my favorites are 5- and 8-pointed stars. From these two shapes can come many fantastic forms. For starters, you will need to extrude and cure the clay, which can then be turned, per directions in the previous tutorial.

TOOLS & MATERIALS

All of the beads in this chapter require these basic tools and materials. Additional items are listed with each tutorial.

⅛-inch (3 mm) mandrels, approximately 6 inches (31 cm) long

> These should be rubberized, per instructions in the Basics chapter (page 28)

A lathe

> For more on lathes, see the Basics chapter, under "Tools" (page 15).

Ceramic trimming tools

> Small circle tools are the best, approximately ¼ inch (6 mm) in diameter or smaller. Buy the best and sharpest (probably the most expensive) ones you can find. They need to have a sharpened edge; a plain wire trimming tool will not work.

Safety goggles

Sandpaper, if you wish to sand and buff your beads

ADDITIONAL TOOLS & MATERIALS

⅛-inch (3 mm) mandrel

> It should be longer than your clay sheet is wide— 8 to 10 inches (20 to 25 cm) is a good length.

A heavy-duty extruder

> The one I use, made specifically for polymer clay, holds about 1 pound (.5 kg) of clay, comes with a variety of die shapes, and can be accessorized with bead corers that will extrude clay with a hole in the middle for beads.

A 3-millimeter bead corer for the extruder

About 1 pound (.5 kg) of polymer clay in your choice of colors

> As usual, I lean towards pearlized clay, for fantastic mica effects on the fabulous fins of these beads.

A rotary tool or electric drill with ³⁄₃₂ (.24 mm), ⁷⁄₆₄ (.27 mm) and ⅛-inch (3 mm) bits

STEP BY STEP

1. Condition your clay to be fairly soft. Roll the clay into one long, continuous sheet.

2. Place your long mandrel at one end of your sheet. Roll up the sheet with the mandrel in the middle, rolling with firm, even pressure to seal the layers together and prevent air bubbles (photo A).

3. If your clay doesn't fit in the extruder, roll it out further with your palms to the desired diameter. Pull the mandrel out of the clay. Insert the clay into the extruder, threading the bead corer through the hole in the middle of your roll of clay (photo B).

4. Affix a star-shaped die to the end of the extruder and screw on the cap.

5. Extrude your clay onto a baking tray in 3-to-10-inch (8 to 25 cm) lengths. Cut the clay next to the extruder and push it off the bead corer from the same end (photo C). You will inevitably squish a certain percentage of your extrusion—don't worry

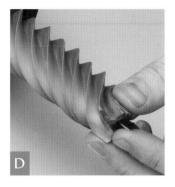

about it. Do not try cutting your beads to length now, as you will squish the fins of the star. Instead, leave longer pieces and cut them after curing.

6. For a twisted effect, take the leading end of the extrusion and twist it before cutting and removing it from the extruder (photo D).

7. Cure the clay in the oven, per the manufacturer's instructions.

8. Remove the clay from the oven while still warm, and cut slightly longer than the desired length of bead with your tissue blade. The warmer the clay, the more easily it will cut; however, it will also distort more easily, which can result in cracks. With practice, you will find a happy medium.

9. Widen the bead hole with your drill. Gradually work your way through the bits, from ³⁄₃₂ (.24mm) to ⁷⁄₆₄ (.27mm) to ⅛ inch (3 mm). By gradually increasing bit size, you will avoid overly stressing the clay, which can lead to cracking.

10. After drilling the hole, mount the clay on a mandrel. (See the Basics chapter, page 27).

11. Turn and finish, as described in Steps 5 through 9 of the Cured-Clay tutorial, on page 77 (photo E).

VARIATIONS

● Use a linoleum carving tool to carve the sides of the fins on a cured and untwisted star extrusion. If you wish, antique the carving with liquid polymer, tinted with oil paints, cure it again, and then turn it (photo F).

● Try covering the fins of a cured-star extrusion with a thin layer of clay, texturing it, curing it, and then turning it. Or try filling in the fins of a cured twisted star extrusion with raw clay, curing, and then turning it.

● Extrude Skinner-blended clay. You can create a blend that varies from one end of the jellyroll to the other, or from the middle to the outside. If you roll up the Skinner blend before the colors have fully merged, you will end up with a fantastic, simple spiral cane.

● Extrude a simple cane. Although it becomes distorted, the results will be interesting.

● Facet your turned and finished beads. I like to sand down two or three sides of the bead with my belt sander, leading to a fascinating interaction between its curved and flat surfaces, interwoven by the fins of the extrusion. If you don't have a belt sander, you can sand by hand, beginning with 80-grit drywall screen. Because these beads can crack around the hole due to the stress of their constuction, try inserting a tube rivet. (See the tutorial on End-Cap Beads on page 86.)

TEXTURED TURNED BEADS

Adding texture to turned forms is like putting skin on bones: It really brings the beads to life. The first of several methods textures the whole bead at once. This method is best for beads with relatively gently curved surfaces, such as peanut shapes. Like the other textured bead tutorials, you can choose to create color contrast in the texture by layering sheets of contrasting colors of clay, or by antiquing the bead with acrylic paint.

TOOLS & MATERIALS

All of the beads in this chapter require these basic tools and materials. Additional items are listed with each tutorial.

⅛-inch (3 mm) mandrels, approximately 6 inches (31 cm) long
> These should be rubberized, per instructions in the Basics chapter (page 28).

A lathe
> For more on lathes, see the Basics chapter, under "Tools" (page 15).

Ceramic trimming tools
> Small circle tools are the best, approximately ¼ inch (6 mm) in diameter or smaller. Buy the best and sharpest (probably the most expensive) ones you can find. They need to have a sharpened edge; a plain wire trimming tool will not work.

Safety goggles

Sandpaper, if you wish to sand and buff your beads

ADDITIONAL MATERIALS

A cured, lathe-turned bead
> It should have complex curves that don't fit your texture channels.

A small amount of raw clay
> Choose two colors of clay to cover the bead. The clay will be layered so that one color defines the raised part of the texture, and the other color, the impressed part.

About 1 pound (.5 kg) of clay
> Use this to create a customizable texture channel. This clay is not baked and is perfectly usable for other purposes afterwards.

Plastic wrap

A flexible RTV or latex silicone texture sheet
> For more on this, see the Basics chapter (page 24).

STEP BY STEP

1. Mount your bead on a rubberized mandrel.

2. Condition the clay for the texture channel. Roll it up into a cylinder and wrap it with two layers of plastic wrap.

3. Roll the bead on the mandrel back and forth along the length of the plastic-wrapped cylinder of clay. This takes a fair amount of pressure. The idea is to create a channel that more or less fits the bead (photos A and B).

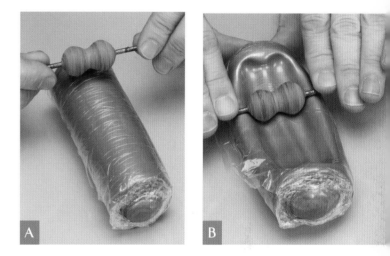

4. Prepare the clay to cover the bead with. Choose a color for the raised portions and roll out a 3-inch (8 cm) sheet on your thickest pasta-machine setting. Roll out a 3-inch (8 cm) sheet of the other color on your thinnest setting. Layer these two sheets together and run them through on a medium setting.

5. Layer the bead with the raw clay. Rough up the surface with 36-grit (or similarly rough) sandpaper. Using the same color that you used for the thick layer in Step 4, smear a thin layer of clay over the bead to insure that the raw clay you cover it with bonds.

6. Take the layered clay from Step 4 and prepare to cover the bead. I use circle cutters to create a piece for each end, and one or more strips to wrap around the middle.

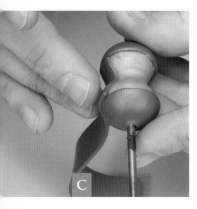

7. Cover the bead with a layer of clay. Place the thicker layer against the bead (photo C). Bring your seams together so that you see only the thin layer of clay on top. Press the clay firmly onto the bead. Use a needle tool to pop any air bubbles.

8. Place your texture sheet on the texture channel.

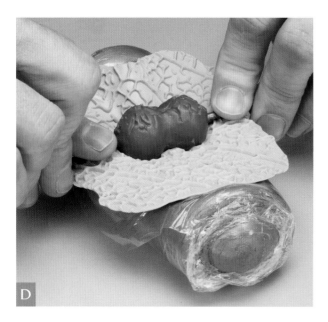

9. Holding your bead by the mandrel, press it firmly into the texture channel so that the texture sheet conforms to all its contours (photo D).

10. Release your pressure and roll the bead slightly forward.

11. Repeat Steps 9 and 10 until the whole bead is textured.

12. Touch up the bead, texturing any untextured surfaces with a tool such as a ball stylus.

13. Cure in the oven, per the clay manufacturer's instructions.

14. Sand and buff to finish.

VARIATION

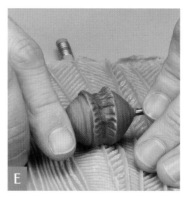

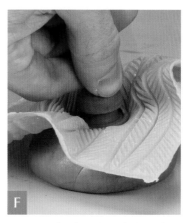

This method can be varied for texturing beads in stages—a good route to go for really complex forms such as those with multiple curves or deep recesses.

With a deeply cut, hourglass-shaped bead, for example, you can layer clay just in the middle, and then place the texture sheet over a properly sized dowel and roll the bead over that (photo E).

Cure the bead and then layer clay over one end, pressing it against the texture sheet, backed with a lump of clay (photo F).

Cure, and repeat for the other end. Multiple-stage curing, the key here, allows you to perform delicate operations on parts of the bead without worrying about damaging the rest.

END-CAP BEADS

These beads combine all of the turning and texturing techniques you have learned so far with the beauty and strength of fine silver. You will be amazed at the ways the two materials intermingle. This multi-stage bead introduces a simple silver clay project and finishes with a beautiful and durable sterling tube rivet. You will also learn how to backfill an entire textured bead and turn it on the lathe to reveal a smooth, patterned surface.

TOOLS & MATERIALS

All of the beads in this chapter require these basic tools and materials. Additional items are listed with each tutorial.

⅛-inch (3 mm) mandrels, approximately 6 inches (31 cm) long

> These should be rubberized, per instructions in the Basics chapter (page 28).

A lathe

> For more on lathes, see the Basics chapter, under "Tools" (page 15).

Ceramic trimming tools

> Small circle tools are the best, approximately ¼ inch (6 mm) in diameter or smaller. Buy the best and sharpest (probably the most expensive) ones you can find. They need to have a sharpened edge; a plain wire trimming tool will not work.

Safety goggles

Sandpaper, if you wish to sand and buff your beads

ADDITIONAL TOOLS & MATERIALS

A dapping block

A small lump of scrap polymer clay

Approximately 10 to 15 grams of silver metal clay

> The amount varies, depending on the size of the bead and the desired size of the end caps. I recommend the clay formulations that shrink the most, as they enable you to capture more detail in a smaller space and to use less silver.

A means to fire your silver clay: a kiln, a torch, or a hot-pot

A latex rubber texture sheet

RTV silicone (enough to make one end-cap mold)

A set of jeweler's files

A turned and textured bead with uncured texture

> The ends of the bead should be dome-shaped (with the same curvature in the dapping block). The bead should be on a mandrel.

A flex shaft (recommended) or drill with a drill bit as large as your sterling-silver tube

A sterling-silver tube at least ⅛ inch (3 mm) in diameter

> The tube should be slightly longer than your bead.

A jeweler's saw and bench pin, or a rotary tool (such as a flex shaft) with a cut-off wheel

> Use one of these tools to cut the sterling tube to length.

Steel dapping punches, 4, 5, and 6 millimeters

A bench block

A jeweler's hammer

STEP BY STEP

Creating the silver clay end cap

1. To make a polymer model, determine how large you want your end cap to be, depending on the size of your bead and personal taste. Select an impression on the dapping block that matches the necessary size. Keep the size of this impression in mind, remembering that your silver clay will shrink in the kiln. My models generally range from about ½ inch to about 1 inch (1 to 3 cm) in diameter.

2. Finding an impression on the dapping block that matches your desired end cap model size, go to the next-smallest size. Fill this with a lump of scrap clay. Pull the clay out, roll it into a ball, and place it on a baking sheet. Cover it with a sheet of plastic wrap, and press it onto the baking sheet, using the selected depression of the dapping block. The plastic wrap will prevent the clay from sticking. Remove the dapping block and plastic, and cure the clay in the oven.

3. After your domed form is cured, cover it with a layer of clay rolled out on medium in your pasta machine. Press the clay firmly onto the cured dome.

4. Place your latex texture sheet over the clay dome (photo A). Remember that you have selected two impressions on the dapping block, and that you have just made a mold of the smaller one. Now, using the larger one (see Step 1), press the texture sheet firmly down onto the clay dome (photo B). Remove the dapping block and texture sheet. You should find a deeply textured dome-shaped model underneath (photo C).

A

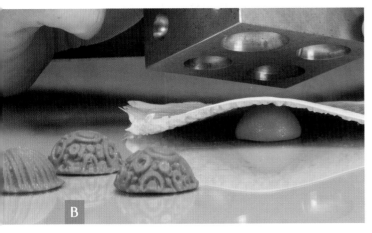

B

C

5. Cure it in the oven.

6. After curing, make a mold. Mix up a small amount of RTV silicone and place it into a depression on the dapping block just a bit larger than your model. Press the model into the RTV, turn it upside down, press it against your work surface, and let it cure (photo D).

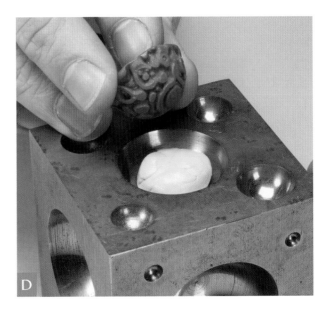

D

7. After the RTV is cured, remove your model. You now have a mold for your end cap.

8. Experiment to photo out how much silver clay to use—just enough to fill in the texture in the mold. None of the RTV should show through the silver clay when it is pressed against the mold, as these areas will develop into cracks. Beyond that, normal strength considerations are not a concern, as the fired silver will be supported by polymer clay. It will function as a hard silver coating, but will not be subject to any particular structural stress.

9. Leaving the mold in the dapping block for support, place the silver clay in your mold, and cover it with a piece of plastic wrap. The plastic wrap allows you to manipulate the silver without having it stick to your fingers or dapping tool.

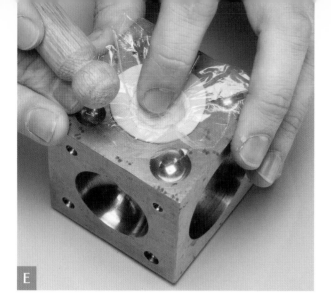

E

10. If you have a dapping tool to fit the mold, use it to press the clay into place; otherwise, do so with your fingers (photo E). If there is excess clay in the mold, squeeze it up above the edge of the mold and remove it. If the clay is too thin in spots, patch those spots with a small ball of clay.

11. Make a small hole in the middle of the end cap. If you can easily make a hole large enough for the sterling tube, do so. Otherwise, create a pilot hole, which you can open up with a file after the clay has dried.

12. Let the clay dry and remove it from the mold. The dapping block as a mold support provides firm support and flexibility when you need it.

13. File the edges of the end cap to clean it up.

14. Using a round file, open up the hole through the middle of the end cap. Remember: It will shrink, so make it just a bit larger than the sterling tube (photo F).

15. Repeat Steps 8 through 14 to create another end cap.

16. Fire your end caps, per the silver clay manufacturer's recommendation.

If the domed shape of your end caps collapses in the kiln, dome them out again by placing each in the dapping block and gently tapping the back using dapping punches and a hammer. Start with a large impression on the dapping block and gradually move to smaller ones.

Assembling the end caps with the polymer bead

1. Slide an end cap over each end of the mandrel, and press the end caps into the raw textured clay of the bead (photo G). Cure the bead in the oven, per the polymer clay manufacturer's specifications.

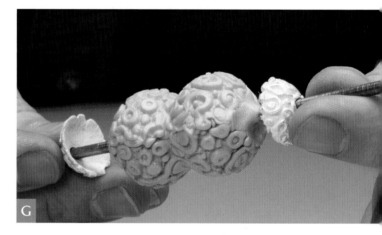

G

2. Select a color of clay that goes well with your bead and wrap the bead in it, end caps included. Press the clay firmly into all of the texture. Pop any air bubbles with a needle tool and press the clay back down.

3. Cure the bead, per the clay manufacturer's instructions.

4. Place the bead in the lathe and turn it, using the instructions in the Cured-Clay tutorial on page 77. Cut down to reveal the pattern defined by the interaction of the textured and the backfilled clay. Cut the ends to reveal the end caps.

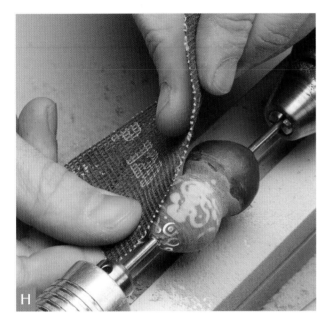

5. Rather than scratch up your end caps with ceramic trimming tools, do your final cutting on the ends, off the lathe, using wallboard screen; this removes a lot of material quickly. Wear a dust mask. If you find that bits of backfilled clay pull out of the texture, patch the holes by pressing raw clay into them and curing again. Repeat the turning process as necessary (photo H). Sand your bead to a fine finish on the lathe. Buff and remove it from the mandrel.

Finishing the bead with a sterling tube rivet

Using a sterling tube rivet is important: It will both hold the end caps to the bead permanently, and provide a smooth, durable finish on the bead holes.

1. Insert the tube into the bead. Allowing it to protrude by 1/16 inch (2 mm) on one end of the bead, mark the tube at 1/16 inch (2 mm) on the other end (a fine-point felt-tip pen works well).

2. To cut the tube with your jeweler's saw, remove it from the bead, hold it on your bench pin, and cut it at the mark. I use a cut-off wheel with my flex shaft, pulling the tube partly out of the bead. Wear safety goggles and, using the bead as a handle on the silver tube, cut it at the mark.

3. File the end of the tube to remove any burrs.

4. Place the tube back in the bead, and center it inside. Place the bead with one end of the tube against your bench block. Place your 4-millimeter dapping punch into the end of the tube. Holding the bead and punch with one hand, tap the punch three or four times with your hammer to begin to open the tube. Turn the bead around and repeat on the other end.

5. Repeat this process next with the 5-millimeter punch. Finish with the 6-millimeter punch. Gently tap down any raised edges of the tube with your hammer, taking care not to dent your end cap (photo I).

RECURSIVE
MOLDED BEADS

Recursive molding allows you to build a library of forms, starting with the smallest and simplest, and building to more and more complex forms. As you go, you can use forms from previous sets to modify the current set. Turn any of these forms into beads by piercing, curing, and sanding them. To shape the clay, you will press it with stretchy latex texture sheets backed with clay cutters or other forms of blank dies. This causes the clay to rise up into the form. When the texture sheet is removed, the clay retains that form, with the texture miraculously wrapped around it. The texture is quite often impressively distorted, sometimes rising into fantastical shapes.

Grant Diffendaffer. *Necklace,* 2007. 18 inches (46 cm) long; focal bead 2 inches (5 cm) in diameter. Polymer recursive molded beads, polymer accent beads and lathe-turned toggle, buna cord.

RECURSIVE BEADS

It is much easier to impress shapes into a sheet of clay than to raise shapes up out of the clay. It is a simple process to make impressions in raw clay, bake the clay, and then create a negative of your impressions by pressing this "mold," or tool, against raw clay. Modify the new piece of clay by making impressions into it. Cure this and make an impression, and suddenly you have a reproduction of the first piece, with forms rising from it that would have been difficult to create in the first piece. Combined with stretchy texture sheets and dies, these mold- and tool-making techniques present a way of carefully and deliberately morphing forms to create dramatic results. It's hard to mess things up.

MATERIALS & TOOLS

Scrap clay to practice

For starters, condition a 12-inch (31 cm) sheet. At first you will just make models, or tools, for making further forms, and thus clay color is unimportant.

A Skinner-blended jellyroll for your final beads

A 10- to 12-inch (25 to 31 cm) Skinner blend should be sufficient. For a smooth transition in your jellyroll, roll the Skinner blend on your thickest setting, cut it into three equal sheets, and stack them one on top of the other. Make sure that your colors match from layer to layer. Run the stacked blend through your pasta machine on a medium setting, putting one color through followed by the other. This will elongate your blend greatly. Decide which color you want in the middle and roll up the sheet, with your palms against your work surface, sealing the layers together, and reducing it slightly. The finished jellyroll should be about 1½ inches (4 cm) in diameter.

Latex gloves or balloons

Latex texture sheets

Refer to the Basics chapter (page 24).

A set of round clay cutters

These cutters should be of the open-ended kind—not the kind with plungers. They should have one blunt edge. The ones I like have one edge that is actually folded over and rounded. You will need only the smaller ones—bead-sized, from about ¼ inch to about 2 inches (6 mm to 5 cm) in diameter. I specify using the blunt edge of the cutter, which gives a more rounded effect to the forms and helps avoid damaging the texture sheets. If your favorite cutters cut through the sheets, try making a protective lip around the cutter with polymer clay. After you get used to the technique, try using various shapes. You can even form your own "cutters" out of polymer clay, by layering two sheets, rolled on through your thickest pasta-machine setting, and cutting a strip 1 inch (3 cm) wide. Turn this on edge, and use it to create any shape you like. Cure the clay and use it in place of the cutters.

A small board

A baking sheet

Dapping punches (useful, but optional)

A dapping block (optional)

Various sculpting tools, ball stylus, etc.

Vinyl protectant in a spray bottle

A toothbrush

Lapidary belt sander (optional)

Rasp (optional)

Sandpaper in the following grits: 220, 230, 400, 600, 800, and 1000

Vibratory tumbler (optional)

BEFORE YOU BEGIN

Each stage in this multi-stage process results in a form that can be used to create one of two things—a bead, or a tool to create further forms. Those forms can in turn be made into beads or used as tools. For our purposes here, I reduce this to the basic process, but suggest variations. I use circular shapes, as they are most simple. As you become familiar with the process, you will likely want to experiment with other shapes of clay cutters. This technique is a great exercise in creativity. Don't concern yourself at first with making finished pieces. If you find you're asking, "What do I do with this now?" the answer is, "Bake it." Put it into the oven, and when it is done, smash it into some raw clay and keep playing. Once you are able to successfully make specific forms with deliberate intention, then you can turn them into jewelry. Until then, just have fun.

There is some preparation to be done before the actual beads are created. Begin by conditioning your clay. Soft clay works quite well for this technique; very firm clay will not.

Roll out a 12-inch (31 cm) sheet of scrap clay on the thickest setting. Cut it into three 4-inch (10 cm) sheets and stack them one on top of the other. Roll with your brayer to seal the layers together. Repeat this process. You should end up with a 2-inch-wide (5 cm) strip of clay that is six layers thick. This provides you with enough clay to create several forms. As you work with the technique, you can vary the thickness. Some smaller forms may require a thinner layer of clay.

STEP BY STEP

STAGE ONE

The first stage in this process is the creating of forms, such as domes and rings. They can be smooth or textured.

Creating Smooth Forms
Domes

1. Place a six-layer stack of clay on your baking sheet.

2. Place a latex glove or balloon over the clay.

3. Put a clay cutter over the glove, with the sharp edge up. The flat area of the hand, not the fingers, is the part of the glove you want to use (photo A).

4. Center your board over the cutter and push down. You will probably have to lean on it to get enough pressure. Press down until you feel the cutter go all the way through the clay. This is a useful time to have a tabletop press like the one I describe in the Basics chapter, on page 16 (photo B).

5. Release the pressure and remove the board, glove, and cutter. Cut around the piece with your hobby knife, if necessary, and remove the excess clay surrounding your cut piece.

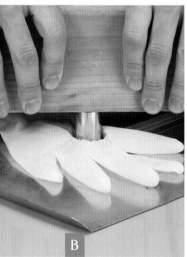

You should have a nicely domed circular piece. If the cutter has cut through the glove, you may have an irregularly shaped piece. Try doubling over the glove next time, and make sure that you are using the cutter with the blunt edge down. You can also increase the number of layers of glove/balloon for more resist-ance and more of a curve to your dome (photo C).

6. Bake in the oven, per the clay manufacturer's instructions.

Rings
Follow the same process as above, but this time use one cutter inside the other, with your sizes selected so there's a ring of space between them (photo D).

Creating Textured Forms

Each section below represents a separate form, and gives you options to explore.

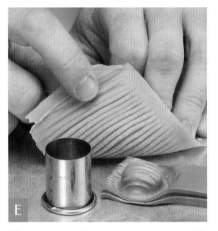

Form 1

The process for creating small domes is the same as for smooth forms, except that you use a latex texture sheet rather than a glove or balloon.

The texture sheet stretches just like the glove. Set up in the same order: clay first, then the texture sheet, the cutter, and the board. Pressing with the board, make several domes with your smallest cutters in different textures. One-quarter to 1 inch (1 to 3 cm) is a good diameter for the small set (photo E).

Form 2

Create a dome, as in Form 1, but when you remove the board, hold the clay cutter in place with your fingers, pressing it against the work surface so the latex doesn't lift it out of place. You will be holding a dome of clay covered by the stretchy latex sheet, and confined on the sides by the clay cutter. Note the shape of the dome beneath the distorted texture sheet. Use a dapping tool, dowel, pen, or your finger to make an impression in the middle of the dome. Release pressure on the cutter, remove the texture sheet, and finish as before (photos F and G).

Form 3

Create a dome, as in Form 1. Remove the board, cutter, and latex. Make a small indentation in the middle of the dome using a dapping tool, tool handle, or any of the smooth clay domes that you created earlier. Finish as before (photo H).

Form 4

Creating a textured ring works the same way as the process for creating a smooth ring (opposite page), except that you use a latex texture sheet. Press down all the way, and you will separate the ring from the inner dome. Press down only partway, and the ring and dome will stay attached to one another.

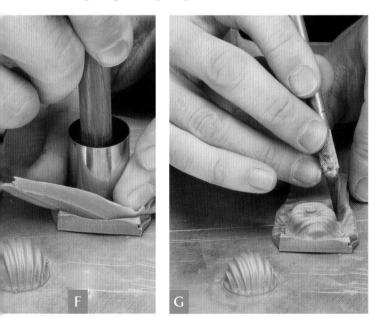

STAGE TWO

For the second stage of this process, make larger versions of the molded forms. In this stage, you will make larger versions of the same basic forms you made in Stage One, but you will modify them with the cured forms that you made in Stage One. Cutters should be large enough to contain the Stage-One Forms, and larger than that by whatever degree you want to add pattern and form. For example, if your Stage-One domes are about ½ inch (1 cm), use 1-inch (3 cm) cutters for Stage Two. At this stage, you can begin to turn out some fantastic, well-conceived, and interesting bead forms. As with the Stage-One Forms, each section that follows represents a separate option to explore.

Form 5

Create several larger domes in the same fashion as Form 1. Experiment with creating impressions in the middle by turning small cured domes or rings

from Stage One upside down and pressing them into the larger domes (use water or some other resist for this part of the process so the domes don't stick together). Modify as you wish with sculpture tools. Notice what happens to the outer edges of the form when you make the impressions. They should bend and flow outward. The result on the outside is to "re-curve" the textured side wall. Cure in the oven (photo I).

Form 6

Spray the clay with water and turn a cured dome or ring upside down on the clay. Put the texture sheet over it, then the cutter, and compress as you did with Form 1. After removing the texture sheet, pick the cured dome out of the raw clay with the point of your hobby knife or your ball stylus. Notice how the texture sheet textures only the part surrounding the impression in the middle. Note the boundary of the two textures and the overall shape of the form. Sculpt as you like, and cure (photos J and K).

Form 7

Create several larger domes in the same manner as Form 1. This time, instead of impressing the domes with Stage-One Forms, inset them with Stage-One Forms. Rough up the back of the Stage-One Form with low-grit sandpaper (you can even drill it out a bit with a flex shaft or drill), so that it has enough tooth to adhere to raw clay. This time, when you press the Stage-One Form into the Stage-Two Form,

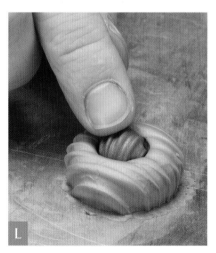

press it upright rather than upside down, leave it there, and cure both in the oven together (photo L).

- If your clay is not doming well or not taking much texture from the texture sheet, it is probably too firm. Try mixing in softer clay, diluent, or other clay-softening products.

- Leaving the molded forms in place on the baking sheet and removing them only after they are cured minimizes your contact with the raw clay and leaves the forms as they popped out of the molding process.

- If you aren't yet making what you consider weird-enough forms, try removing them from the baking sheet while raw and stretch and distort them. You can even form them into hollow domes that are well suited for creating hollow-form beads.

- If your raw clay sticks to your cured clay when you are molding a form, try using vinyl protectant rather than water as a resist.

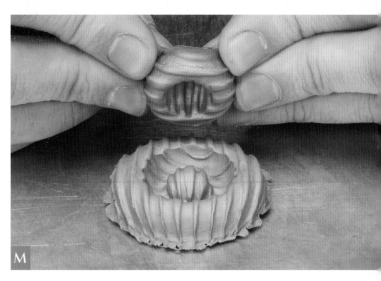

STAGE THREE

Stage Three builds on Stage-Two Forms by using them to create further forms or molds, which are then altered and used to create variations on Stage-Two Forms. Depending on how large the forms are from the previous stages, models made using Stage-Two Forms as tools can be quite large.

Form 8

Create another form using Stage-Two Forms in the same fashion in which they were created. Making a Stage-Three Form large enough to contain the impression or insertion of a Stage-Two Form might make Stage-Three Forms too large (photos M, N, and O). If this is the case, try Form 9 or Form 10 on the following page.

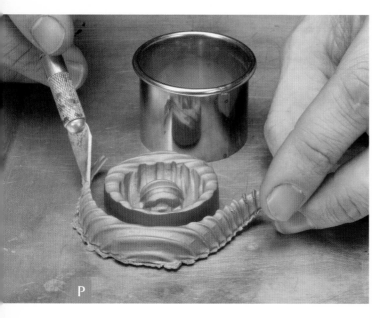

Form 9

Use only a portion of the model you create, with a Stage-Two Form as a tool. Try making an impression of a Stage-Two Form and then using smaller clay cutters to select only part of it, discarding the cut-off part outside the cutter. You can do this with just the cutter, or you can first lay a latex texture sheet over the impression which, as you know by now, will further modify the form. Cure in the oven. This piece can now be used as a tool to create a Stage-Four Form (photo P).

Form 10

Create a mold from a Stage-Two form by spraying it with vinyl protectant as a release. Scrub it into any recesses with a toothbrush. Press the form into a piece of clay large enough to make a complete or partial impression of the form. Remove the form and modify the impression with your sculpture tools. Cure in the oven. Try doing at least three molds from the same form and then altering them in different ways.

STAGE FOUR

There's more!? Well, just a bit. This process can actually be carried out ad infinitum, but there are two more essential variations. You can now use a Form 10 Stage-Three mold to create shapes that will be variations on the Stage-Two Forms they were made from. You can also use the tools from Form 9 to modify forms in the manner of Forms 5, 6, and 7.

FROM FORMS TO BEADS

As fun as it may be to make molds and models, the time will come when you'll want to make a finished bead. The first step is to use some pretty clay. One of my favorite options is to use a slice of a Skinner-blend jellyroll (see the "Before You Begin" section of this chapter, on page 93). Any stage can be used to create a finished bead. Simply substitute your intentionally colored clay for the scrap clay. Pierce your bead while it is still stuck to your baking sheet to minimize distortion during the piercing process (photo Q).

I also like to cure the bead without removing it from the baking sheet, again, to minimize distortion. This means a lot of sanding to get the nice rounded back I like. To remove this much material and really shape the beads, I generally use my lapidary belt sander. Alternatively, a rasp will quickly remove large amounts of material. In lieu of either of these methods, you can remove the bead from the baking sheet while raw (use a palette knife or tissue blade) and carve the back of the bead roughly to shape with a tissue blade. Finally, you can simply leave the bead on the baking sheet and sand down the edges by hand after curing it. Sand the rest of the bead, per your preference for either a shiny or a matte-finished bead.

You may feel a bit overwhelmed after reading and maybe even after attempting everything in this chapter. "What on earth is the purpose?!" you may cry. "Are these molds or are they models? Are they tools, beads, or just weird-looking lumps of clay?" It is my intention, and my hope for you, to blur the distinctions. The beauty of this process is that there is no clear delineation between working on a finished piece of jewelry, working on a tool that is just a means to an end, and squishing a lump of clay for the pure joy and educational value of it. I hope that it helps you to learn the crucial artistic lesson of listening to the process and letting the clay express itself, instead of trying to squeeze it into the rigid mold of your preconceptions. Making something you have never imagined will greatly increase your ability to imagine things you have never made, and then go on to make them.

Grant Diffendaffer and **Kirsten Anderson**. *Necklace,* 2007. 19 inches (48 cm) long; focal bead 1½ x 1¾ inches (4 x 4 cm). Polymer recursive molded beads, polymer lathe-turned beads, polymer lathe-turned toggle, black onyx, multi-strand nylon-coated stainless steel wire.

MOLDED
HOLLOW-FORM BEADS

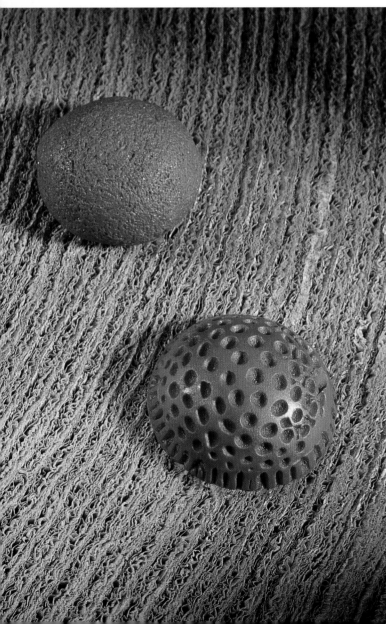

Polymer clay, a wonderfully light material, can be used to make large beads that are deceptively light. If you want to make even lighter beads still, you can build them over an armature of aluminum foil, specially designed lightweight polymer clay, or— lightest of all—air.

There is something captivating about a bead that weighs almost nothing. This tutorial teaches you to make a hollow-form bead using room-temperature vulcanizing silicone mold-making material and variations of some techniques you learned in previous tutorials in this book.

Grant Diffendaffer. *Beads,* 2006-2007. Polymer molded hollow-form beads; textured.

HOLLOW BEADS

To explore these hollow beads, start off by making a model, then a mold of the model, next a rough hollow bead, and finally, a finished bead with a decorative surface.

MATERIALS & TOOLS

Soft scrap clay for the model
A balloon or latex glove
A set of clay cutters
A small board
Two-part RTV silicone mold material
   Use the putty variety, which involves mixing
   equal parts.
Colored clay for the finished bead
   Because the bead will be hollow, strong clay
   is important.
220- and 400-grit sandpaper
A bead mandrel
A rotary tool, such as a flex-shaft machine
A diamond bit in the same diameter as your mandrel
A needle tool
An 80-grit sanding sponge

STEP BY STEP

Creating a Model

To make a model of the form that you want to re-create in hollow fashion, assemble a bead from a domed sheet of clay and a flat backing. The techniques that started off the recursive mold-making chapter are ideal for creating such shapes.

1. Create a stack of soft scrap clay about ½ inch (1 cm) thick and measuring about 2 x 2 inches (5 square cm). Roll the stack with your brayer or roller to seal the layers together. Place it on your baking sheet.

2. Lay a balloon or latex glove over the clay.

3. Place one of your clay cutters over the rubber layer, dull side down (photo A).

4. Using the board, press the cutter through the clay (photo B).

5. Remove the cutter and rubber layer and trim away excess clay (photo C).

6. Cure the model in the oven.

Creating a Mold

Now make a mold from the model you made.

1. Remove your model from the baking tray, and clean up any rough edges with a piece of 400-grit sandpaper.

2. Mix together equal parts of the silicone mold-making material to form a ball large enough to encase the dome of the model (not the base).

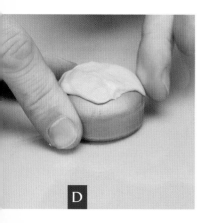

3. With the model on your baking tray, press a layer of RTV silicone around it that is about ⅛ inch (3 mm) thick. Create a small tab of the silicone that protrudes away from the model. Allow the silicone to cure, per the manufacturer's instructions (photo D).

4. Create a sheet of scrap clay about ¼ inch (6 mm) thick (two layers from your thickest pasta-machine setting). Press it over the silicone, leaving the extended tab of RTV uncovered. This scrap clay will form a rigid support for the flexible mold (photo E).

5. Cure it in the oven.

Creating the Hollow Armature

After you've made the mold, create the hollow armature.

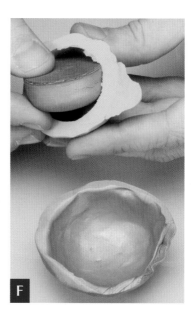

1. After the mold support has cured in the oven, separate the model, mold, and mold support. (Remove the mold from the support; then, flexing the mold, pop out the model.) (photo F)

2. Replace the mold in the mold support.

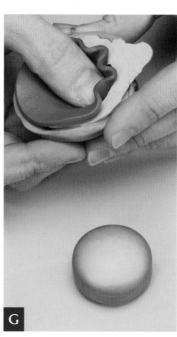

3. Roll out a sheet of clay on your thickest pasta machine setting. Press it into the mold, taking care to press out any air under it. Use latex gloves or a sheet of plastic wrap if the clay sticks to your fingers and pulls out of the mold (photo G).

4. With your clay blade, trim off excess clay around the edge of the mold (photo H).

5. Cure it in the oven.

6. After the clay has cured, remove it from the mold.

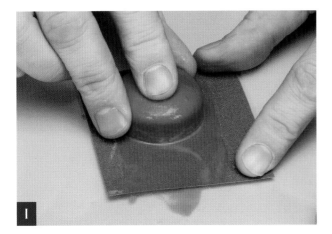

7. Place the 220-grit sandpaper on your work surface, and sand the bottom edge of the domed surface until it is flat (photo I).

8. Using your rotary tool with the diamond burr, cut notches in the edge of the bead where you want your holes to be. Make the notches large enough that the mandrel fits down into them (photo J).

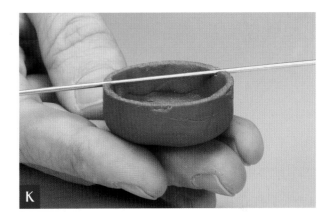

9. Place the bead mandrel in the notches that you cut, and gauge whether they need to be larger. The mandrel should sit flush with the edge of the clay (photo K).

10. Roll out a sheet of clay on your thickest pasta-machine setting and double it over. Roll it with your brayer to seal the layers together. The results should be slightly wider than your domed form. Place it on your baking sheet.

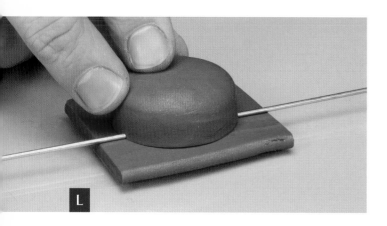

L

11. Place the domed form with the mandrel on top of the sheet of clay, centering it in the middle (photo L). Remove the dome and leave the mandrel.

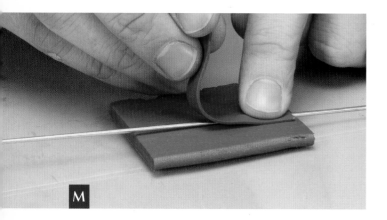

M

12. Roll a small sheet of clay on a medium setting. Cut a strip about ½ inch (1 cm) wide and lay it over the mandrel (photo M).

13. Press the strip of clay around the mandrel.

N

14. Place your needle tool on the sheet of clay so that when you put the dome on it, it sticks out (photo N). Later, you'll remove the needle tool, leaving a vent hole that will prevent the bead from cracking in the oven.

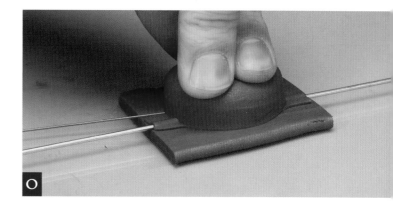

O

15. Place the dome on the clay so that the notches fit over the mandrel. Press the dome down gently but firmly into the clay, forming a good seal (photo O).

16. Trim around the edges with a hobby knife and remove excess clay. You don't have to make a perfect edge, as you can fix it up after it is cured (photo P). Remove the needle tool, leaving a tiny vent hole.

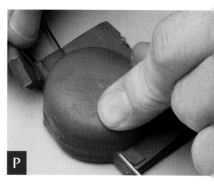

P

17. Cure the bead in the oven.

Covering the Bead
with a Decorative Surface

As you have learned by now, there are many ways of
patterning polymer clay. This bead now provides a
blank canvas for your artwork. Experiment with
covering it with canework, mokume gane veneers,
ghost image veneers, and texture. In this tutorial I
give the bead a simple porous texture. For more
complex sculptural textures, try using molds of
recursive molded beads.

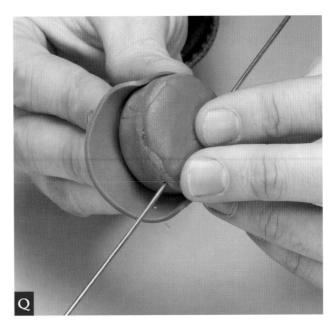

1. A sanding sponge is one of my favorite texturing
tools. As it comes from the store, however, it's difficult
to use effectively. It is best to remove a slice from one
edge, giving you a thin strip that is easier to manipulate. Also, without the absorbent sponge behind it,
you can exert more pressure through the textured
surface. Stand the sponge on end and remove the
slice, using sawing motions with a clay blade.

2. Remove the mandrel from the bead and trim off
any rough spots with a hobby knife. Replace the
mandrel in the bead.

3. Cover the bead with a medium-thick layer of
colored clay, and smooth out the surface with your
fingers (photo Q).

4. Texture the bead using the strip from the sanding
sponge (photo R).

5. Cure it in the oven.

MANDREL-FORMED
PILLOW BEADS

Grant Diffendaffer. *Necklace,* 2007. 18 inches (46 cm) long; largest bead 7 inches (18 cm) long. Mandrel-formed polymer pillow beads (ghost-image veneer, carved, backfilled), polymer accent bead and toggle, buna cord.

Perched at the base of the neck, no collar fits better than one constructed to a solid form such as a necklace mandrel. Its heavy metal body lends itself to making inflexible pieces like collars or torques. It can also be used to create interlocking beads that, because they were formed on the same mandrel, echo the unified design of their more solid kin.

This tutorial involves a steel necklace mandrel, used by jewelers to hammer metals to fit the human form. The mandrel serves as a removable armature to support the form of the raw clay in the oven.

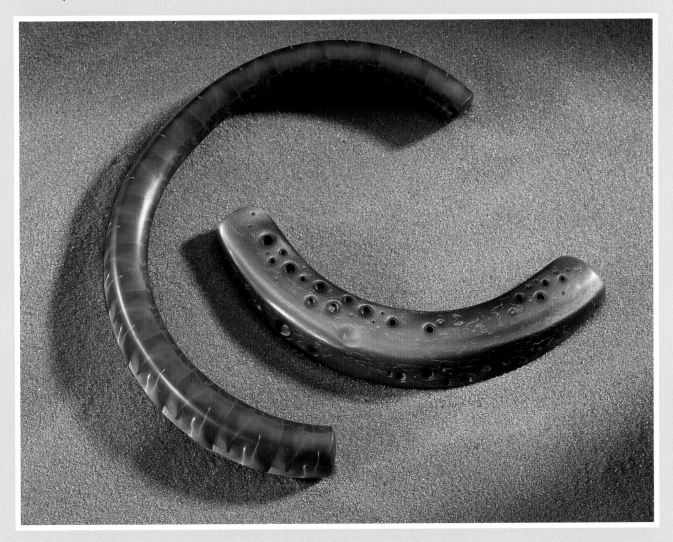

MANDREL-FORMED BEADS

These beads are similar to the pillow beads on page 55 in that they are hand formed over a shaped core bead and cured in multiple stages.

MATERIALS & TOOLS

Clay

The amount you need depends on how big your beads are. You may want to use clay for the core bead that matches the color of the surface clay, as it may be exposed during the finishing process.

A 10- or 12-inch-long (25 or 31 cm) bead mandrel made from ⅛-inch (3 mm) steel wire welding rod

⅛-inch (3 mm) diameter synthetic rubber cord, 20 inches (51 cm) long

This is available from many bead and jewelry supply businesses as well as from distributors of O-rings. Great cord to string polymer on, it will help you form the beads.

Vinyl protectant spray

This is the same substance you use to shine the plastic surfaces in your car.

A number-10 taper-point clay shaper

A cast-iron necklace mandrel

I use a small one. The size you use will affect the measurements, but you should have an easy time making any adjustments.

Abrasive tools for shaping the beads

These include a belt sander, rasps, abrasive wheels, drywall screen, and sandpaper.

Sandpaper, starting at 320 or 400 grit

BEFORE YOU BEGIN

The first challenge in making a bead like this is to make a hole that follows the curves of the bead. So let's start with the hole. You will make a long, flexible tube bead over synthetic rubber (buna) cord and build the beads around it.

STEP BY STEP

1. Begin as if you were rolling tube beads, as described in the Basics section (page 27).

2. Roll a 9-inch (23 cm) sheet of clay around the bead mandrel. When it is as long as the rod, cut it in half. Set aside half and continue rolling the other half. When this is as long as the rod, cut it in half again and remove both pieces. You will use only one piece here, but it is easier to roll accurately if you start with more clay.

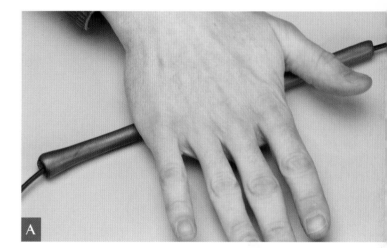

A

B

3. To transfer one of the smaller tubes to the rubber cord, use a paper towel, and wipe the cord with a coating of vinyl protectant, which prevents the clay from sticking. Reduce the tube as if you were using a bead mandrel to make tube beads. Roll it back and forth with your palms, coaxing it with your fingers when it gets thinner (photo A). Occasionally stretch the cord, pulling from both ends at the same time, to free up the clay tube wherever it is stuck (photo B). To reduce the thin tube precisely, grasp the tube between the

C

fingers of each hand, and simultaneously twist and stretch it, letting your fingers slide over the surface and stroke the clay (photo C).

4. Stop rolling when the tube is about 18 inches (46 cm) long. Trim off any uneven ends to leave the tube exactly 17 inches (43 cm) long.

5. Turn the round tube into a triangle by pinching

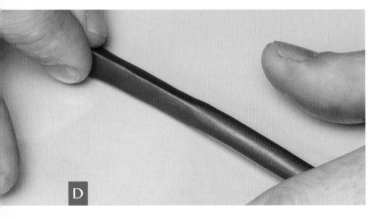

D

it along its length—similar to the process of turning a round cane into a triangular one. Pinch with your thumb and forefinger to form two sides, simultaneously pressing it against your work surface to form the third (photo D).

6. Roll out a 17-inch-long (43 cm) sheet of clay in the same color as your tube, on your thickest pasta-machine setting. Use a straight edge and blade to trim the edge of the sheet if it is not even. Lay

E

your triangular tube of clay and cord straight along the smooth edge of the sheet, approximately ¼ inch (6 mm) from the edge. Use your blade to make a parallel cut in the sheet ¼ inch (6 mm) on the other side of the tube (photo E).

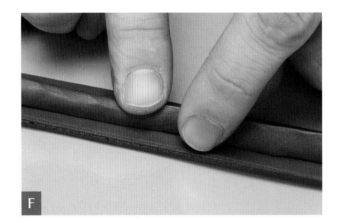

F

7. Press the tube down into the clay, starting along the top of the tube, and flattening out the top edge of the triangle. Continue by pressing down along the edges, applying firm pressure with your fingertips to stretch the clay out and down into the bottom sheet, blending them together (photo F).

8. Use heavy finger pressure to smooth and blend the clay along the length of the bead that is gradually taking shape (photo G). Don't be overly concerned with uneven edges along the work surface, as they will be covered with another layer of clay. Rather, concentrate on smoothing out the clay. You don't want any gaps left to become air bubbles that might later create gaps or weaknesses in the bead.

G

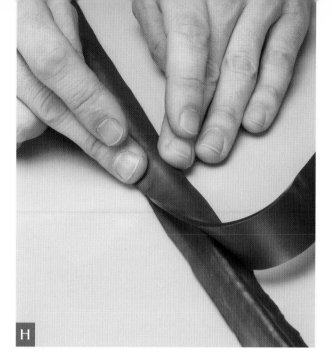

H

J

9. Cut a strip of clay from your sheet that's 17 inches (43 cm) long and 1 inch (3 cm) wide. Use it to cover the bead, centering it along the spine, and pressing it down on either side (photo H). Take care to squeeze out any air, and press the clay layers firmly together. Use your needle tool to pop any air bubbles and squeeze out any air. At this point the bead really begins to take shape. If there is anything you want built into the form, do so now. You can also add clay once it is on the mandrel. Refinements in form can be made to the raw clay on the mandrel, as well as to the cured clay afterwards.

I

10. Grasp each end of the rubber cord and stretch it, decreasing its diameter so that you can pull it back and forth in the tube to ensure that it doesn't stick to the clay and can move freely (photo I).

11. Use a painter's palette knife to remove the tube from your work surface. Hold the two ends of the tube and pull them together to form a circle. Keep the bottom of the tube flat against your work surface.

12. Put the tube on the necklace mandrel. Center it around the neck with the two ends of the tube meeting behind the neck. Press it onto the surface and mold its form as desired. Add or remove clay at this point if you like. Trim it with a hobby knife, keeping in mind that this is just a core bead, and that you can make more delicate refinements after it is cured. Also remember that it will be covered with a decorative layer and will grow in the process. Last, remember to preserve the thickness of the layer of clay immediately surrounding the cord. You can press on this layer, but don't make any sharp impressions that might focus any flexing pressure and create a crack (photos J, K, and L).

K

L

13. Cut the bead into as many beads as you like. To make a cut right over the break of the shoulder, I tie a string around the mandrel, under the shoulders, and over the top. This gives me a good line through the same part of the necklace on each side. With the slicing corner of your tissue blade, gently slice against the mandrel into the bead until your blade comes to rest on the rubber cord within (photo M). Remove your blade and slice from the opposite side to meet the cut you just made. When the blade reaches the cord, roll it forward across the cord to join the other cut. Don't slice the cord. (It is easy to cut above and on both sides of the cord.) Leave the small piece of clay right under the cord; this piece will easily and cleanly break after the curing process, as you see in photo O.

14. After cutting out the form of the beads, you can further sculpt and refine them (photo N).

15. Cure the whole assembly in the oven. The heavy steel mandrel will take a while to reach the required curing temperature. Curing, as always, depends on the manufacturer's instructions, but I leave it in the oven for well over an hour, and then let it cool completely in the oven to prevent cracking.

16. Remove the beads from the mandrel. Break the small remaining joints between the beads by flexing towards the inside, or joined side, of the necklace. Flexing in this direction will help ensure that you make a clean break (photo O).

17. Shape the core beads with drywall screen. Fine sanding is not necessary at this point because you want a rough surface that raw clay will adhere to. At a minimum, clean up the ends and edges of the beads with the drywall screen, and use it to rough up the surface of the rest of the bead.

Covering the Core Beads with a Decorative Layer

The beads in this tutorial were made with a ghost-image veneer, made by impressing texture into a double layer of pearlized clay, rolled on the thickest setting of my pasta machine. I sliced away the raised texture and ran the clay back through the pasta machine to smooth it out. While these look beautiful with a mica veneer, they are also very striking with canework and would lend themselves well to other surface decoration schemes.

18. The beads are now finished one at a time on the mandrel. To start with, string a bead on the rubber cord and tie it into place in its appropriate position on the mandrel.

19. Smear the front surface of the bead with a thin layer of clay. After smoothing it with the clay shaper, apply a decorative layer. I use a layer from the thickest setting on my pasta machine to avoid stretching my pattern too much and to give myself leeway in sanding the finished piece: The thicker the outer layer, the more I can sand away before sanding all the way through. Wear latex gloves to prevent smearing your patterns or leaving fingerprints. Press this layer gently and firmly into place, bending it around the curves of the bead. Remove any air bubbles by pushing them out towards the edges. Use a needle tool to pierce any bubbles. Especially with mica-shift techniques, keep your manipulation of the surface to a minimum to avoid disturbing your carefully created patterns. Trim away all excess clay with your hobby knife (photo P).

Tip

Part of the beauty of this process is the ability to make long, curved beads. However, I recommend cutting the large bead into at least two or three to reduce the stress the bead body is subject to during the normal course of wear. Still, feel free to experiment by making beads as long as you like. You can even make a torque, or a solid necklace with no bead hole, that is designed to flex just enough to fit around a neck. If necessary, you can tie the two ends of the cord together to keep the ends of the necklace properly situated on the mandrel. Remember to cut the ends of the necklace short enough to leave room for a clasp, cord, or any other beadwork that you want to add to complete the necklace in the back.

20. Smear a thin layer of raw clay to the back of the cured core beads. Smooth it out using the clay shaper. Apply a medium-thick sheet of clay, which can be decorative, to the back of the bead. Press it firmly but gently into place, removing any air bubbles.

21. Using the edge of the cured bead as a guide, trim away the excess clay with a hobby knife (photo Q).

22. Cure it in the oven, per the manufacturer's instructions.

23. Finish the beads with sanding and buffing. You will probably want to start sanding with 320- or 400-grit sandpaper, depending on how much shaping you need.

VARIATION

Carve and backfill the surface of the bead to create another layer of visual interest (photos R and S).

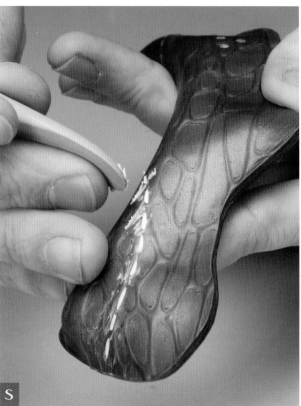

GALLERY

KATHLEEN DUSTIN

Village Women, 1998
Each, 1½ x 1½ x ¾ inches (4 x 4 x 2 cm)
Polymer clay, gold leaf; millefiori, multilayered, multibaked, sanded, polished
PHOTO BY GEORGE POST

KATHLEEN DUSTIN

Odalisque on Her Pillows, 1997
20 x 6½ inches (51 x 17 cm)
Polymer clay; sculpted, cane work
PHOTO BY GEORGE POST

Tornado Beads, 2005
Each, 3 x 1 inches (8 x 3 cm)
Metallic polymer clay, translucent
polymer clay, gold leaf, embedded
glitter; Skinner blends, layered,
carved, backfilled, sanded, polished
PHOTO BY ROBERT DIAMANTE

Peeking Face Pebble Beads, 1999
18 x 3½ inches (46 x 9 cm)
Polymer clay, colored pencil, gold leaf;
multilayered, baked, sanded, polished
PHOTO BY GEORGE POST

SARAH SHRIVER

Forest Collar Necklace & Earrings, 2006
Beads, 1¼ x ¾ inches (3 x 2 cm)
Polymer clay, brass, citrine and apatite beads; cane work, millefiori
PHOTO BY GEORGE POST

Blue/Green Bracelet, 2006
Beads, 1¼ x ¾ inches (3 x 2 cm)
Polymer clay, rubber cord, brass beads;
millefiori
PHOTO BY GEORGE POST

Fish Beads, 1999
Beads, ¾ x ¾ inches (2 x 2 cm)
Polymer clay; cane work
PHOTO BY GEORGE POST

CYNTHIA TOOPS

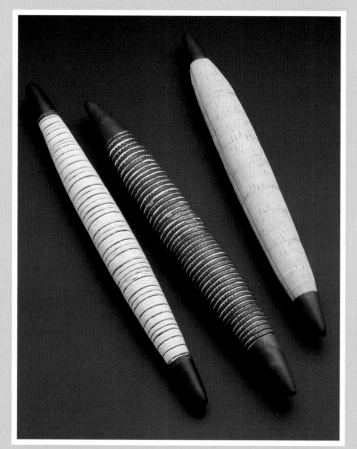

Untitled, 2006
2½ x 1 x 1 inches (6 x 3 x 3 cm)
Polymer clay; embellished with hollow
cane slices
PHOTO BY ROGER SCHREIBER

Untitled, 2003
Each, 6½ x ⅞ x ⅞ inches (17 x 2 x 2 cm)
Polymer clay, clay patina; carved, rebaked
PHOTO BY ROGER SCHREIBER

Ball Sampler, 2006
Largest bead, 1 inch (3 cm)
Polymer clay, glass, felt, ceramic, sterling silver;
cane work, micromosaic, tile mosaic
PHOTO BY ROGER SCHREIBER

JEFFREY LLOYD DEVER

Asymmetrical Flair, 2006
2½ x 2½ x ⅞ inches (6 x 6 x 2 cm)
Polymer clay, plastic-coated copper wire, anodized
niobium cable; hand fabricated, form-built hollow
forms, carved, backfilled
PHOTO BY GREGORY R. STALEY

The Catch, 2003
3 x 2¼ x ½ inches (8 x 6 x 1 cm)
Polymer clay, anodized aluminum wire, anodized
niobium cable; form-built hollow forms, wire-wrapped
basket form, hand fabricated, drilled
PHOTO BY GREGORY R. STALEY

Oasis, 2005
3½ x 4 x ⅜ inches (9 x 10 x 2 cm)
Polymer clay, glass-head pin, anodized niobium cable;
hand fabricated, form-built hollow forms, drilled
PHOTO BY GREGORY R. STALEY

ELISE WINTERS

Autumn Cinch Bracelet, 2006
2½ x 7½ x ¼ inches (6 x 19 x 1 cm)
Polymer clay, crazed acrylic
PHOTO BY RALPH GABRINER

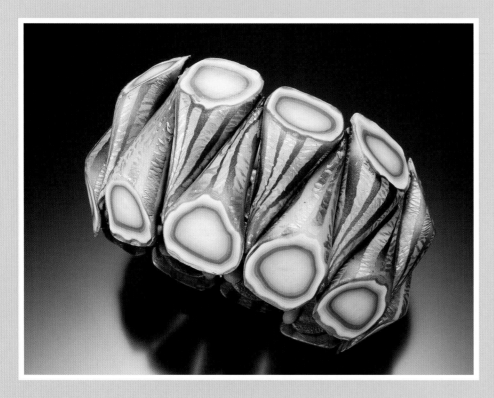

Skinner Inner Cinch
Bracelet, 2006
1½ x 7½ x ¼ inches
(4 x 19 x 1 cm)
Polymer clay, crazed acrylic
PHOTO BY RALPH GABRINER

Nine Sautoir, 2004
Length, 64 inches (163 cm)
Polymer clay, crazed acrylic, gold, vermeil, silver, mica
PHOTO BY HAP SAKWA

CELIE
FAGO

Untitled, 2006
2½ x ⁷⁄₁₆ inches (7 x 1 cm)
Polymer clay, paint, precious metal clay, red and yellow brass, sterling silver, copper, 22-karat gold slip, 24-karat gold kum boo, glass beads; formed, fired, incised, hand fabricated, constructed, fused, strung, attached
PHOTO BY ROBERT DIAMANTE

Incised Lizard Pendant, 1999
3⅞ x 1⅝ x ¼ inches (10 x 4 x 1 cm)
Polymer clay, paint, antique beads; formed, image
transfer, inlay, incised, strung
PHOTOS BY ROBERT DIAMANTE

DAN CORMIER

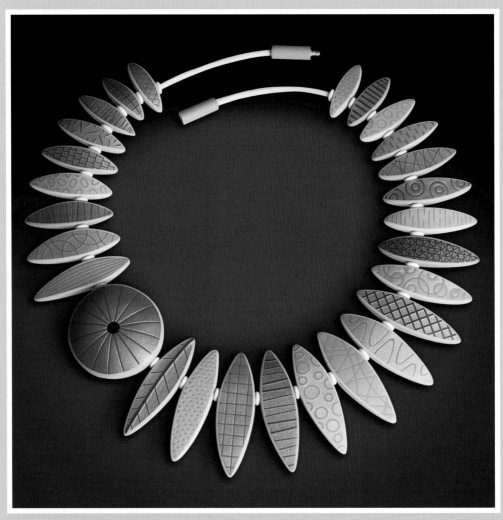

Botanical Necklace, 2005
Length, 22 inches (56 cm)
Polymer clay, rubber cord and o-rings, barrel
clasp; carved, die formed, draped bead
construction, Cormier veneer
PHOTO BY ARTIST

Botanical Pin, 2005
2½ x 2½ inches (6 x 6 cm)
Polymer clay, sterling silver; die formed,
Cormier veneer
PHOTO BY ARTIST

Cutting Edge Beads, 2005
Largest, 1½ x ½ inches (2 x 1 to 4 x 1 cm)
Polymer clay; die formed, Cormier veneer
PHOTO BY ARTIST

DEBRA
DE WOLFF

Untitled Bracelet, 2006
4¼ x 4¼ x 1¼ inches (11 x 11 x 3 cm)
Natural brown alpaca, polymer clay, glass seed beads, copper beads, vintage sequins,
crystal beads; felted
PHOTO BY LARRY SANDERS

Untitled Necklace, 2006
20 x 3 x 1¼ inches (51 x 8 x 3 cm)
Merino wool, dye, polymer clay, glass seed beads, memory wire; felted
PHOTO BY LARRY SANDERS

JUDY
KUSKIN

Tears of the Rainforest, 2005
Length, 20 inches (51 cm)
Polymer clay, sterling silver, fine silver
PHOTO BY ARTIST

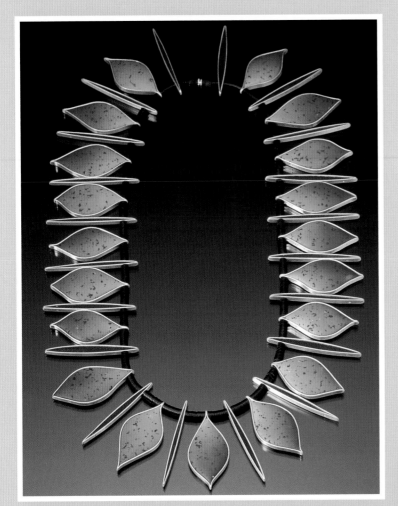

Untitled, 2006
2 x 8½ inches (5 x 22 cm)
Polymer clay, sterling silver
PHOTO BY DOUG YAPLE

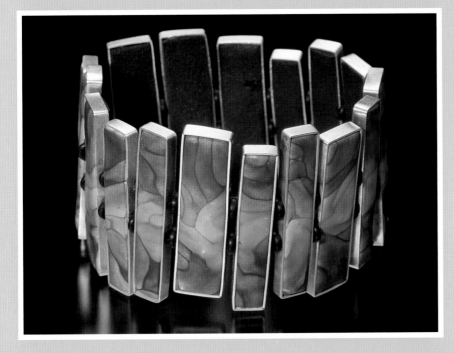

Untitled, 2006
Length, 20 inches (51 cm)
Polymer clay, sterling silver
PHOTO BY DOUG YAPLE

LINDLY
HAUNANI

Twisted Lei, 2006
18 x 3 inches (46 x 8 cm)
Polymer clay; altered cane work
PHOTO BY DAVID TERAO

Asparagus Crown Bracelet, 2006
4½ x 8 inches (11 x 20 cm)
Polymer clay, elastic
PHOTO BY DAVID TERAO

Pod Leis, 2006
18 x 1¼ inches (46 x 3 cm)
Polymer clay; altered cane work
PHOTO BY DAVID TERAO

WENDY
WALLIN MALINOW

Candy Links, 2006
Length, 30 inches (76 cm)
Polymer clay, acrylic paint; hand fabricated, inlay, cane work
PHOTO BY COURTNEY FRISSE

Jacks and Chicken Feet, 2006
1½ x 3½ x 1 inches
(4 x 9 x 3 cm)
Silver clay, polymer clay,
steel, acrylic, paint; inlay,
sgraffito, buffed
PHOTO BY COURTNEY FRISSE

Winter Cameos, 2006
1 x 8 x ½ inches
(3 x 20 x 1 cm)
Polymer clay, sterling silver,
vintage tins; hand fabricated,
buffed
PHOTO BY COURTNEY FRISSE

KAZUYO KONO

Goldfish Bead, 2005
1 x 1¼ x ¾ inches (3 x 3 x 2 cm)
Polymer clay; cane work
PHOTO BY ARTIST

Goldfish Bead, 2004
1 x 1¼ x ¾ inches (3 x 3 x 2 cm)
Polymer clay; cane work
PHOTO BY ARTIST

GLOSSARY

Backfill: The practice of filling an impression or cutaway in cured clay with raw clay and then curing the clay again. Backfill can either be made level with the surface of the clay, or just used to color the inside of an impression. It is an excellent way to add colored accents to your beads.

Cane: A tube or rod of clay with a pattern inside that is revealed when you slice a cross-section of the cane. Canes are derived from an ancient glass-working technique known in Italy as millefiori, or "thousand flowers." Canes enable the artist to create highly detailed patterns.

Curing: The process of properly hardening polymer clay by applying heat.

Durometer (or Shore Durometer): A measure of hardness used for plastics. It is relevant to photopolymer platemaking in that the pattern resin commonly used for making texture plates is typically about 95 Shore A Durometer. A softer and more flexible version appropriate for rubber-stamp making measures 35 or 45 Shore A Durometer.

Ghost imaging: A mica-shift technique that consists of stamping or impressing with texture pearlized clay containing mica particles. The texture is cut away to leave a smooth surface that appears to have a three-dimensional texture. The effect looks like a handmade hologram.

Ingot: A brick or block of pearlized mica clay with the reflective mica particles deliberately organized to create a mica-shift effect or pattern. A plain ingot is made of sheets of conditioned mica clay stacked one on top of another. A more complicated ingot can be formed by cutting an ingot apart and re-assembling it in another fashion.

Latex: A natural rubber product used for making molds. I use latex to create stretchy texture sheets.

Leaching: The practice of removing the softening plasticizer from a thin sheet of clay by pressing it between two sheets of paper. The plasticizer soaks into the paper, and the clay thereby becomes stiffer and more manageable.

Mica: A flaky mineral that gives many pearlized clays their shimmery qualities. Mica particles, which act like little mirrors in the clay, can be manipulated by distorting and physically reorganizing the clay body in different ways.

Mica shift: The result of organizing mica particles in the clay so that the color of the clay visually shifts between light and dark shades as the clay is moved. This effect can be subtly and dramatically controlled using what are known collectively as mica-shift techniques, which include constructing ingots and making ghost images.

Millefiori: The Italian technique (meaning "thousand flowers") of working with canes of glass to create patterns. This has been translated into a polymer technique by the same name. It can be used to make a flowerlike pattern or, indeed, an infinite variety of other pictures and patterns.

Mokume gane: A Japanese metalworking technique that can be approximated with polymer. It translates as "wood-grained metal" and involves layering different colors of metal, distorting them, and cutting into them to reveal the patterns within.

Necklace mandrel: A cast-iron bust made for shaping metal for jewelry. It is used as an armature for polymer clay in the Mandrel-Formed Pillow Beads chapter (page 108).

Pattern resin: High-durometer photopolymer resin used to create texture sheets for polymer clay, as well as printing plates, dies, and similar industrial products.

Photopolymer resin: A polymer resin of honey-thick consistency which hardens under exposure to ultraviolet (UV) light. It is used to make texture plates, rubber stamps, printing plates, and other products.

Post-exposure solution: A solution in which photopolymer plates are exposed to UV light at the end of the manufacturing process. This process removes remaining tackiness on the surface of newly formed plates.

Realign: To cut an ingot at an angle between the bright and dark sides. The effect is to transform an ingot with a bright top and bottom and four dark sides into one with only two dark surfaces and four that shift, appearing bright from one angle and dark from the opposite.

Room-temperature vulcanizing silicone: A two-part mold-making material that cures into a flexible rubber when the two parts are mixed. It is available in both liquid and putty forms. All references to room-temperature vulcanizing silicone, RTV silicone, or just RTV in this book refer specifically to the putty form of RTV, which is mixed in equal parts.

Veneer: A thin decorative sheet that is applied to create the surface of a bead.

ABOUT THE AUTHOR

Grant Diffendaffer has been working with polymer clay since 1993. His introduction to the material came by way of several intricately caned beads that he stumbled across while still a philosophy student at the University of Puget Sound in Tacoma, Washington. Soon after, a friend brought him some of the clay and helped precipitate a shift from his left-brained studies to a life in art.

Grant's beads, jewelry, sculpture, and decorative art display a keen sense of color, composition, and form, as well as a meticulous attention to detail. His work has been shown in numerous juried craft shows, galleries, and exhibits.

Grant works from a studio at his home in Canyon, California, which he shares with his three-legged cat Jalebie and his partner, jewelry artist Kirsten Anderson. When not creating or finding inspiration for his art, he stays busy traveling the globe to teach his unique techniques to others.

CONTRIBUTING ARTISTS

ACKNOWLEDGMENTS

I have been thinking about writing this book for some time, and the actual doing of it was a much bigger process than I ever imagined. I don't know how I would have done it without the love, understanding, and jewelry-making skills of my wonderful partner (and soon-to-be wife), Kirsten. Her support was indispensable.

I owe so much to the polymer clay and bead communities. Thanks to all the hardworking people, many of them volunteers, who have organized all the classes I have taught over the years. Thanks to everyone who has ever come to one of my classes or purchased my work. You are the ones that make it possible for me to live out my dream of being a working artist. They say that buying someone's work is the ultimate compliment, but thanks also to all of those whose compliments were merely verbal—you have made my day many times.

Thanks to the incredible artists who have shared their work for this book. I am honored to be in your company here.

I have great appreciation for Kaya Westling and Kelly Fordan, who have so generously shared with me this little slice of heaven we call home.

I am grateful to my parents, who have always been there for me as I navigate the trials and tribulations of life as an artist.

Thanks to Lark Books and everyone there who has helped this book come into being. To Terry Taylor, who first encouraged me to submit a book proposal. To Nicole McConville, who saw the promise in this book and helped to get the process rolling. To Pat Wald, who diligently tracked down the answers to complicated questions for me. To Valerie Shrader, my intrepid editor, who endured my deadline struggles and helped me wrangle out all the difficult issues involved with creating this book. To Fran Ross for going through the book with a fine-toothed comb. To Nick Elias for applying his dedication and skill to the tutorial photography. To Nathalie Mornu, art director Megan Kirby, bead photographer Stewart O'Shields, and everyone else who helped to make the book a thing of beauty.

I owe much thanks to all of the artists who came before me, and those who have come up beside me, for pushing the boundaries of this new material, polymer clay, with imagination and devotion. Thanks lastly to all of you who read this book and turn to pick up the clay—we need your creativity!

Grant Diffendaffer. *Necklace,* 2007. 18 inches (46 cm) long; largest bead 1½ inches (4 cm) long. Polymer beads (lathe-turned and textured), polymer accent beads and lathe-turned toggle, buna cord.

INDEX

Grant Diffendaffer and **Kirsten Anderson**. *Necklace,* 2007.
19 inches (48 cm) long; largest bead 1¾ inches (4 cm) long.
Polymer beads (carved from ripple-striped and blade-bruised
ingots), polymer lathe-turned toggle, black onyx spacers,
multi-strand nylon-coated stainless steel wire.